IF
I
COULD
CONVINCE
YOU
OF
ONLY
ONE
THING

IF I COULD CONVINCE YOU OF ONLY ONE THING

essays

Zelda Leah Gatuskin

Cover and book design by Studio Z, Albuquerque, NM.

Previous publication credits:
The Introduction, "Art and Religion and Science and Reason," was originally presented as a lecture for the American Humanist Association in 2010. The essay "Bill Baird, My Hero and My Friend" was published under the title "Bill Baird: Wounded Warrior Battles On" in the Winter 2012 issue of *Free Mind*, a publication of the American Humanist Association. The essays in Parts 1 and 3 were originally published in the Humanist Society of New Mexico *Newsletter*. The essays in Parts 2 and 4 were originally published on Zelda Gatuskin's blog, "The Tree." Essays have been edited for inclusion in this collection.

First Printing, 2018
ISBN: 978-0-938513-61-2
Library of Congress Control Number: 2018936493

AMADOR PUBLISHERS, LLC
Albuquerque, New Mexico, U.S.A.
www.amadorbooks.com

It is not necessary that we believe in each other's beliefs, so long as we believe in each other. —ZLG

IF I COULD CONVINCE YOU
OF ONLY ONE THING

Contents

Part 4. We All Deserve Better
[Essays from "The Tree" blog, 2013 – 2016]

Appendix

About This Collection

As an introduction to myself and the short and medium-length essays contained in the four parts of this collection, I have included a rather lengthy text. It is adapted from a talk I delivered to the Humanist Society of New Mexico in 2009, and then in expanded form at the 2010 National Conference of the American Humanist Association. (HSNM is a chapter of the AHA.) It marks the inception of all of the writing that follows; as well, it was a significant factor in my being recruited to leadership roles with both groups.

"Art and Religion and Science and Reason" begins with some background about my Jewish upbringing, my life as a creative artist, how I became a publisher, and my serendipitous path to humanism, the Humanist Society of New Mexico and the American Humanist Association. My central thesis is that the Fine Arts have been neglected in contemporary humanist thought and activism in favor of the Sciences. Probing for the cause of this Science-Art imbalance while I prepared my case, I hit a nerve that has yet to be quieted—the realization that the chauvinism of Science over Art is of a piece

1

with the overall, all-pervasive, chauvinism that marks Western society. With that clarifying idea, my feminist zeal was reawakened. Fortunately, the AHA's Feminist Caucus (now called the Feminist Humanist Alliance) was there to receive me.

Not long after that 2010 conference and my discovery of the AHA's feminist adjunct, I was nominated for president of the Humanist Society of New Mexico. Since that tends not to be a contested position, I was duly elected to a two-year term; then my other arm was twisted, and I was elected to a second term. One of my reasons for deciding to accept, twice, such a demanding task was this: In order to improve the status of women, we need more women in more leadership positions. That means that when an opportunity comes around for a woman to lead, she ought to accept. So, I practiced what I preached, and the experience gave me the courage to keep on preaching.

The essays of Parts 1 through 4 are chronological within each section, and the parts themselves are roughly sequential or overlapping. The writing spans the period from January 2011 to mid-September 2016.

During the four years of my HSNM presidency, I wrote a column every month for our *Newsletter*. Parts 1 and 3 contain a selection of those essays. They were written to inform and motivate our members, and to engage newcomers with a practical, positive example or explanation of humanist philosophy.

At this same time, I was also increasing my involvement with the AHA, leading to my stepping in to fill a

Feminist Caucus co-chair position from mid-2012 through mid-2014. This resulted in my creating a blog titled "The Tree" for my feminist-humanist essays and related media analysis. I have gathered the most significant of these into Parts 2 and 4 of this collection.

I continued the blog series into 2016; but as the U.S. presidential election neared, I found myself unwilling to contribute more words to the avalanche of opinion and analysis coming from every quarter. I had repeatedly offered strong critiques of our popular culture, media and politics. On the subject of women's rights, I felt there was nothing more to say— Except, maybe, "I told you so," and no one wants to hear that.

Now, with the passage of time, I find that the writing is still relevant. The issues are certainly still close to my heart. In combining selections from my newsletter pieces with the blog posts, I notice that they are all spin-offs, one way or another, from my "Art and Religion and Science and Reason" presentation. In lending my voice to the feminist-humanist movement, I have continued to draw from my studies in visual art and media literacy to expose the underlying themes, motives and methods of our ubiquitous mass culture. My approach to the essays, as with the talk, has been that of an artist; my goal, to demonstrate how the Arts allow us to explore our complex and conflicted human nature—and the necessity of doing so.

The new essay in this collection serves as my Conclusion. Whereas the title essay is an appeal for personal empowerment ("If I Could Convince You of

Only One Thing, It Would Be This: Value Yourself"), the concluding essay, "A Philosophy for Everyone," offers a practical, positive approach to getting along better as a society.

Finally, I have included as an Appendix the complete text of the Universal Declaration of Human Rights, which was a topic of one of my early humanist essays.

All of the opinions expressed in this book are my own and not offered on behalf of either the Humanist Society of New Mexico or the American Humanist Association. I am deeply grateful to both groups for valuing my voice and entrusting me with responsibilities that required me to be more organized in my thinking and direct in my communications. I was honored to work among many caring, accomplished and influential people, from bona-fide celebrities, to community movers and shakers, to an array of dedicated volunteers quietly contributing their skills and energy to bettering our world. I am deeply appreciative of everyone who encouraged, challenged, educated and inspired me along the way. I hope this collection will inspire in turn.

Introduction

Art and Religion and Science and Reason

a presentation delivered at the National Conference
of the American Humanist Association
June 5, 2010, San Jose, California

Art and Religion and Science and Reason
June 2010

I am dedicating my lecture today to Harry Willson. Harry was my friend and mentor for twenty years. In 1989 he agreed to publish my first novel, *The Time Dancer*, and from that time forward I was effectively apprenticed to Harry. He taught me everything I know about publishing and much of what I know about writing. In 2006 we converted Amador Publishers, the press which Harry and his wife Adela Amador founded, into an LLC and I became co-owner and managing editor. The object was for me to effect a peaceful takeover of the company in order to keep our titles in print, provide an outlet for Harry's literary works, and let Harry and Adela retire.

Even before we came up with this plan, Harry had designated me as his literary executor. I remember the discussion well. "I'm adding a codicil to my will," Harry told me, "so that you will take charge of all my unpublished manuscripts." To which I replied, "You can will me anything you want. But no dying!" We had many good laughs about that over the years, especially while we were working on his book *Myth and Mortality*,

7

and right up to the week before he died of cancer in March of this year.

Harry had been giving me little pushes toward the humanist community for a number of years. He'd ask me to come along to meetings with him when he spoke to our local Humanist Society, the Friendly Philosophers and other groups. I'd take care of selling books and get to meet his gang, which comprised many local activists, teachers and philosophers. When we reorganized the company, Harry convinced me that Amador Publishers should officially declare itself a humanist press. It fit with the mission Harry and Adela had stated from the beginning: "dedicated to peace, equality, respect for all cultures and preservation of the biosphere." There was no question that the local humanist community was our audience, consistently supporting Amador Publishers over the years and welcoming Harry's thoughtful and challenging writings.

The funny thing was that although I felt in agreement with the philosophy Harry and his friends espoused, I had never fully subscribed to the mantle of humanism. Now I was going to run a humanist press. How was I going to pull that off?

Our local Humanist Society president got wind of our plans and suggested I personally join the AHA and HSNM, now that I was going to be at the helm of Amador. I sent in my dues and began receiving lots of literature about humanism. I started attending our monthly lecture meetings regularly, not just when Harry spoke. I was impressed by the presentations from our local activists and philosophers, and I was touched by the kindness and caring of these people, who took me into their fold and bolstered me during a time of sadness and upheaval. So, all of you of the humanist community are part of the gift that Harry willed me, and I'm deeply grateful and committed to carrying on our work.

My first task has been to articulate for myself what makes me a humanist, and how to frame that in the context of running a humanist press. It has not been so easy, and I have often felt contrary along the way. All those years that I tagged along with Harry to the HSNM meetings, why did I not join? I agreed with much of what I heard, was heartened by the depth and intelligence of the discussion, and enjoyed being in the company of other freethinkers. So I needed to figure out what was off-putting to me, and if I might have something constructive to offer to correct that, versus just staying away.

This talk is the result of that inquiry. It starts with Saturday mornings, which is when our chapter meetings are held—because my first task was to take care of the knee-jerk stuff. Specifically, I have this ingrained resistance to popping out of bed on Saturday morning to attend "meetings" of any kind, and I bet some of you can guess why.

In childhood, Saturday mornings meant going to *shul*—synagogue. Up until the age of nine, that entailed a rather long car ride to get to the more orthodox temple —a perplexing proposition given that driving at all on the Sabbath was forbidden, like a variety of other things, some of which we did and some of which we didn't.

Like it or not, on Saturday mornings my sisters and I were roused from bed and put into uncomfortable clothes, and made to look nice and behave nicely and mingle with other kids like us, Jewish kids. Then we did it all again on Sunday morning for classes and activities which were not held on the Sabbath because of the proscription against writing or "creating" of any sort.

On Sundays, Hebrew lessons and religious instruction were followed by choral rehearsal and Israeli folk dancing. There was a chorus and a dance group for each of several age brackets—grade and middle schoolers, teens and adults. In addition, the numerous Jewish holidays and festivals we observed created opportunities for a variety of arts and crafts projects, theater skits and pageantry. This was my early experience with the arts.

Looking back on it, I did have fun and find fellowship at *shul* and—especially with regard to the folk dancing—I was introduced to activities which to this day provide some of my greatest pleasures. The problem was that even the creative outlets were offered within narrow parameters. Subject matter was always along cultural or religious lines: We only did Israeli dances. When we had arts and crafts, we made *Seder* plates and *Hanukah* menorahs. We sang Hebrew songs, acted out the Purim play, and put on cabarets to raise money for Israel. But on the Sabbath, the day of itchy dresses, after a long week of coloring within the lines at public school, God commanded that I shouldn't be allowed to create at all!

I didn't think of myself as much of a threat to God's creative powers. I sort of thought that God, being such a good creator, and having created me with the peculiar collection of traits I possessed, might actually approve of me making use of them. Besides, we were allowed to read and think on the Sabbath, to nap and dream. Even as a child, I understood that although activities of the hands could be curtailed, the ultimate creative process could go on, might even be unstoppable. My mind had a mind of its own.

Remembering my early years, certain events stand out as having accelerated my growing self-awareness and awareness of the world. My aunt came to live with us following an illness. The stylish, self-sufficient operator for Western Union, with the gracious southern drawl—a model of the liberated woman of her times—had become a reclusive shadow of her former self. It was not a good situation, and the grown-ups worked it out so that she moved to her own apartment. Strangely, it was not her moving in that rocked my world, it was her moving out. The room that my aunt had vacated became mine. For the first time in my life I was not sharing with an older or younger sister. Privacy. A place to think my own thoughts.

"Zelda, you come down here right now!"

But just because I got to be alone sometimes didn't mean I would be left alone. There was still school, Hebrew school two afternoons a week, *shul* on Saturdays, Sunday school, family activities. It was downright oppressive. I was rejecting religion as the

11

basis for actions and self-definition, and I was rejecting the secular gods at the same time. I noted that my father got up before dawn, shaved, dressed in a suit and tie and rode off to work, not to be seen again until late afternoon. Sometimes he worked in the evenings at a card table with his charts and slide-rule. Mom wanted her girls to be educated and have careers. I was supposed to want to be something. In order to make a living.

"What do you want to be when you grow up?"

This question plagued me. To get everyone off my back, I declared that I would be an artist. A poet, a painter—the medium was beside the point. Now, if the question was about earning a living, that was an entirely different matter. I would be an artist because I was an artist—I felt I could be nothing else. When the time came to work, then I would find a job. That wouldn't be a problem, because artists can do many things.

That was it. That was my plan at age nine.

As I described, my introduction to the arts began in the context of Jewish culture. Fortunately there were good arts programs in the public schools I attended, and I was able to pursue visual art, music and theater in a secular setting as well. Further, my father's mother was an artist and craftswoman, and she mentored me from an early age. And finally, I benefited from proximity to the Arden community of north Delaware. Being welcomed into this diverse secular, artistic community was empowering and liberating. It was not a repudiation of the Jewish community and their activities. It felt like a natural progression—to start within nurturing cultural confines, and "grow up" socially and artistically into a widening and more diverse circle.

Arden was founded in 1900 by sculptor Frank Stephens and architect Will Price. Based on the economic philosophy of Henry George, Arden was organized as a single-tax, arts and crafts, garden-city, in which the land is held in common. Originally known as a summer home for artists, musicians and theater people, Arden continues to offer arts activities all year long at the Guild Hall, there on the village green.

Through the Arden Folk Guild, my sisters and I added international folk dancing to our Israeli dance. And I participated in the Arden Theater Guild.

My plan, such as it was, carried me through high school, where I took every arts class I could, and gave up on math and science as soon as they would let me.

I went up to Emerson College in Boston as a dramatic arts major, then switched over to visual arts. I stopped out a year to take studio classes at art schools in the area. But something was lacking in all of this theory and practice of art: the science.

I needed to know *why*. Why do we see what we see the way we see it? How do I know that what I see is what you see? How much control do I really have over what you see? Where do the principles of visual design come from? Without knowing *why*, art would be just another set of rules to take on faith.

I returned to Emerson to pursue an interdisciplinary

course of study between the Fine Arts and Education departments, and received one of the first degrees given there in Visual Communications. My fine arts courses were primarily in art history and the new visual literacy curriculum. My education classes dealt mainly with cognitive development and perception—work that has evolved into the field of cognitive science. This was what I had been seeking—the objective basis for the fundamentals of design that have been repeatedly expressed throughout human history right up to today. Our creative output may have become digital, disembodied, but our aesthetics are still rooted in physics and physiology.

While in Boston, I met Frank—now my husband— then a student at the Boston Conservatory. Frank had experienced a similar progression from sacred to secular in his life as a musician, starting with church choir, of course. Then his dad took him to the barbershoppers group. Adolescence brought folk music, rock 'n roll, and all the popular styles Frank chose to sample at his own discretion.

But when Frank and I ended up at our respective colleges in serious pursuit of our art forms, what do you know? We found ourselves thrown back to that old time religion, the primary context in which the art of past times had been created, or at least preserved.

From the earliest jot on a cave wall to the soaring spires of Gothic cathedrals, art is associated with the spiritual needs of the human psyche. Whether an expression of awe, an attempt at direct communication with the divine, or a depiction of a significant insight or observation, Art, by definition, stands apart from the mundane tasks of physical survival. As civilizations advanced and humans became more prolific with their symbol making, we find writing and images of an obviously functional nature: accounts, biographies, laws and directives. But to us, today, it still looks like art. For these artifacts reveal sophisticated aesthetic tastes and skilled methods of production: form and function.

The craftsmen and innovators of past centuries did their work in the context of sacred art because they were supported by church commissions. These are the works we study in art history. The Jews do not have a long tradition of representational art, since the making of idols is forbidden. And any art they did create, as with the art of other minorities and women, has been subsumed by the dominant Christian culture of its day, and by the mainly Christian arbiters of culture who until recently took charge of documenting and critiquing such things. Therefore, like every student of Western art, I am steeped in the iconography of the church. Jesus, Mary and the Apostles are my old college buddies.

In art and music history class, we study the arts on their march forward to the present. We see the sacred element fall away and secular interests and aesthetics begin to predominate. There will always be religious art, but high art outgrew the old contexts.

The title of Tony Hileman's essay on the AHA web site caught my attention: "Living on the Creative Edge of our Culture." He states, "It was the humanist impulse of the Renaissance that refused to accept the status quo and freed us from the shackles of authoritarianism, recognized our human abilities and responsibilities, and moved us forward toward where we are today." Hileman doesn't say *who* was living on the creative edge of culture during the Renaissance, but we know who: the artists. We know them as artists, anyway, because of the impact of their visual imagery. But, they were men (mostly) of the arts *and* sciences—"Renaissance men." Much of their innovation involved the observation and depiction of the world around them. They perfected methods for conveying volume and depth in two dimensions, of foreshortening and perspective; they understood the properties of light and shadow. They were striving for a rational depiction of a rational world.

For a time, Frank and I literally owed our sustenance to the church. As in the days of old, the church provided work. Frank had assorted church music jobs, and when we lived in Boston he worked for the Andover Organ Company, helping to fix and tune old tracker pipe organs for churches all over New England. I even got a job out of the deal one summer, restoring the paint and gold leaf to a set of case pipes.

Yet Art and Religion have always had an uneasy association. He who pays the musician gets to pick the music and lead the dance. Much as we welcome the paying work, artists inevitably feel constrained by this. We wonder what we might produce under less fettered circumstances, and we crave the chance to find out.

As for our employers, retaining artists and musicians to further the glory of God and Church is like keeping tigers at the circus. They want to attract an audience with the raw power of our creative energy, while also trying to tame that energy to their service. Like the tiger, the well-trained artist may perform on command, but we do not submit. Art is inherently subversive of religion. Imagine: our audience might be swept away beyond the confines of religious thought to experience—actually experience—a true oceanic feeling independent of dogma.

Not only is the artist a freethinker, but she suggests that anyone might be. When the artist exerts creative will to make something where there was nothing before, he competes with God. And when he succeeds, and manifests that creative potential with indisputable skill, he risks outshining the Higher Power. Mozart pens music that actually sounds like a heavenly choir. Michelangelo converts a hunk of rock into a "Pieta"—a work of spiritual import, which betrays the artist's interest in pure material physicality: the flesh of Jesus' broken body, the fabric of Mary's gown, not to mention the marble and muscle that went into creating it.

Artists practice art the way others practice religion. We are freethinkers *and* we are religious. We are even prone to proselytize—as I am doing today. We think everyone should spend some time with the arts. Which brings me to my critique of the humanist movement from an artist's perspective.

When I began getting to know humanism and considering how and why I might define myself as a humanist, I found the philosophy to be a naturally good fit. Further, I felt that what made it a good fit for me also made humanism a good fit for other artists: the spirit of exploration, civic-mindedness, open-mindedness, rejection of authoritarianism. I concluded that the practice and study of the arts is fundamentally a humanist endeavor, and I wondered why the arts received such short shrift in the humanist literature. It seemed to me that the Arts could and should be as rich a source of instruction in humanist principles and the skills we need to promote them as are the Sciences.

We've already touched on the Renaissance. In every era the great minds who contribute to the flowering of human knowledge about the universe, nature and humanity itself are typically "Renaissance" types—people with a diverse and deep interest and knowledge that spans both Science and Art. Musicians, painters and scientists revere Mozart, Leonardo and Einstein not *respectively*, but *equally*. But so much of what comes across in the humanist argument has to do with Science and Reason. This brings me around to my original concerns:

Is art unreasonable?

Is art unscientific?

Is art optional?

Is art so utterly subjective that it has nothing to offer but "activities" and sentimental cultural attachments?

Or maybe art is too elitist, too reliant on "talent" to

find its place among non-artists, except in the context of something to be sold and consumed.

I would like to dispel all of those notions and propose that artists and humanists have a lot to offer each other. That the Arts and Sciences belong together.

The arts and sciences, quite simply, encompass everything. This is the place of freedom, where every kind of thing can be looked at in every kind of way. If we desire to understand ourselves and our world, and to improve the human condition, then all things human must be open for discussion, including all of the products of the human imagination.

It has always seemed obvious to me that formalized religion—combining theater, music, arts and crafts, poetry, storytelling and dance—is a necessary (though some might argue, misdirected) response to our human capacity and desire for artistic expression. But the therapeutic value of creative activity is often negated or relegated to the side by religion, with its balance sheet of compulsory practices and taboo behaviors. In the religious realm, we don't just make stuff up and trick ourselves into believing it for a time; we may base decisions on it and impose it on others.

Whether a religious myth began as a playful flight of fantasy or an insightful metaphor about human nature, once it has hardened into dogma, it blocks the way of anything new and becomes a dead end for the true artistic temperament. This is why I say that artists are humanists by nature. We must constantly re-observe and

19

re-interpret everything. We are not content with other people's answers. That will sometimes put us at odds with science. Even though we appreciate the scientific method and apply it in our work, we are no more interested in a scientific authority than we are in a religious one. Science has its myths and fictions too. But the imaginative side of science is self-critical—actually eager to find and examine new evidence, re-examine old evidence, and revise "the current fantasy" accordingly.

Art is true and real of the moment. It does not demand your total allegiance. The fate of the world or the fate of my soul does not rest on the work of art.

Art can feel extraordinarily dangerous for this very reason: It doesn't have any apparent unified agenda. It smacks of anarchy. It is a threat to capitalism because it is not concerned with money. It is a threat to religion because it is not concerned with god. It is a threat to science because it is not concerned with reason. It is out there on the frontier of human consciousness looking for a way to break through to the language we haven't invented yet—the language that will make us one, or make us free, or make us sane.

Yet, definitions of humanism seem loath to give art its due. Instead we have science and reason. You may have noticed that this phrase doesn't win me over. It's not that I want to be unreasonable, or to be around unreasonable people, or to dispose of reason as a value. But I object to the implication that science has the corner on reason. I also object to conflating reason with morality. For example, the Humanist Society of New

Mexico publishes a brief definition of humanism in each monthly HSNM *Newsletter* that begins with this statement: "Humanism is an ethical philosophy that derives its principles from science and reason rather than from theology."

My response to this is that reasonableness is itself subjective or at least situational. And science, unfettered, is hardly any more moral than art, or religion. Science too has a playful element: "Let's do it because we can." It may be ruled by pure curiosity, or driven by chauvinistic impulses: "We humans know best, we humans are in charge of the world."

Does being a humanist really mean I'm not to care about other species? Am I supposed to place my faith in science and thereby sanction the nonstop torture of animals in the name of research? Is breeding a rat, torturing it and then killing it in the name of Science really more enlightened and reasonable than slaughtering a sheep as a sacrifice to God? How about breeding, torturing and killing a million creatures, fifty million— every year?

Are you getting mad at me yet? Art can be pretty emotional, but I don't think it's unreasonable.

I don't want to demote science. I would just like to restore it to that earlier place where Art and Science were inseparable, each informed and inspired by the other. That would be something different from the statement which appears on the inside front cover of every issue of *The Humanist*, though here, at least, art made it into the first sentence: "Humanism is a rational philosophy informed by science, inspired by art, and motivated by compassion."

I like the compassion part. But notice that art inspires, while science informs. In this equation, Art has actually been relegated back to the Art and Religion realm. Art is going to be the catch-all for this whole irksome bag and baggage of "culture" with its unfortunate preponderance of mystical and mythical iconography. Plus, art can absorb the continuing troublesome human inclination to mystical experience and supernatural belief.

Science is going to be the daddy, forging bravely— but reasonably—ahead, and art can be the mommy, nurturing and unconditionally accepting the unruly human heart as it "grows up" to embrace rational secularism.

That's an uncomfortable analysis for a philosophy that intends to be egalitarian and enlightened. But I'm just saying how it feels, to me, to read those words about what humanism is and isn't, and why I chafe against them.

The chauvinism of science over art feels very much to me like traditional male chauvinism. Right off the bat, we have science paired with reason, implying that art might be unreasonable—and therefore unreliable for the long haul—in the same way that women have been discounted as being too emotional to be effective thinkers or leaders. Art is something to look at, preferably something pleasing, like a woman. Art is the muse; science is the achiever. Science is a player in politics and the economy. The scientist is someone with a good job at a university or a lab, or a chemical engineer like my dad, someone who is paid to do work which society considers necessary. Artists are expected to starve. We will do our work for love with or without pay, just like moms and wives and daughters have traditionally—and if we should actually make money, serious money, we will be thought of as sell-outs and prostitutes.

Art and Science used to be a team, a marriage of equals. They'd both had their dysfunctional relationship with religion and progressed to the secular milieu, where they met in anatomy class, courted over experiments in perspective and were wed to the perfected intervals of Bach and Beethoven.

Somewhere along the line Art and Science broke up. At least that's the rumor. And it didn't start that long ago. Once Albert Einstein had ushered in our age of abstract mathematical thought, science seemed to race ahead of average mortal comprehension. Soon the pace of technological advances also began leaving us behind, and it continues to do so. Even as we grow more sophisticated in applying the fruits of technology, the tools we use are more and more a mystery to us. Those who know how to program and repair our devices are nothing less than gurus.

The impact of this transition on the arts has been huge. Technology has made art more accessible, more diverse. It disseminates more art by more artists to more people than ever before. It has made everyone an artist, and everyone a critic, while throwing into question the very meaning and purpose of art. Art is in crisis. Frustrated by religion and cast aside by science, the fine arts—still starving, alternately indulged and ridiculed as a nonessential frivolity—are an easy target for that pimp, the corporate media.

Not so long ago science was under attack by religious fundamentalists and losing ground fast. Scientists, educators and reasonable people of all stripes came together to defend the place of science, and the standards for science teaching, in public education. The modern attack on the arts, which had endured and survived the wrath of religionists for centuries, has been more prolonged and subtle.

We don't perceive the corporatization of culture as a movement or a philosophy, but as the result of economic forces. When arts education is stripped from the schools, it's presented as an economic necessity. We don't perceive capitalism as a kind of religion, with its own fundamentalist wing out to convert, absorb or kill anything in its path. We may suppose that only an indifferent economy determines that art is to be relegated to extracurricular activities or, for those who can afford the luxury, private instruction. But today's extreme polarization into "sides" on every issue, from the most urgent to the most trivial, and extending to our very comprehension of what is objectively true, is evidence that we surrender art to the marketplace at our own risk.

We have a highly sophisticated media applying art in the service of propaganda, mainly to do with economic interests. And we have a receptive audience: your basic human beings, bubbling with creative energy, craving an outlet for expression, a drama of some sort in which to participate, actually or vicariously. Having been conveniently dumbed down and long deprived of any really stimulating or elevating fare by the very same media machine that plays to those unfulfilled creative needs, this audience is ripe for manipulation.

The language of visual communication is everywhere, so all-pervasive in both work and play that we hardly notice. We are responding to it whether we understand its dynamics or not. In this environment arts education is more than a diversion or a dispensable cultural romp. The teaching of visual and media literacy is as essential to the development of critical thinking skills and the improvement of social discourse as any science class. In fact, it is science. Art and Science.

Certainly the folks who make the TV shows, billboards, cereal boxes and pop-up ads are up to date on all of the latest findings in cognitive science. They would like to be in complete control of our synapses. Advertising is the high art of our age. Art moves us emotionally, and so it is used to manipulate thoughts, decisions and behavior. Advertising is also the low art of our age. Where once there were crafts and decorative arts to enhance the beauty of objects, now we live in a visual world that consists primarily of advertising and branding. Challenging the corporate media is essential for our future as a civil, functional society, and it is also essential for artists and the concept of art itself.

Commercialization, contrivance—everything today is appropriated to the service of selling and profit. Artists, pushed to the brink of destitution, buy into it. Being able to produce and broadcast something ourselves and make it go viral on the Internet feels a lot better than being ignored by the elite gatekeepers of popular culture. But we're playing into their hands even as we feel we've gotten around them. We lose our sense of what we're doing and why by accepting hits, views, clicks, tweets and friend requests as the measure of our success.

I implied earlier that science is prone to excess, and I think that art is too. Art is making stuff. We add to the problems of society when we are overly productive and not sufficiently selective about what goes out into the world. Remember that old phrase "the rat race"? It has never been more apt. We (and not just artists) are being run through a maze which appears to offer many rewards and pleasures along the way, but ultimately saps our energy and diverts each person's particular sort of creative drive into something recognizable by the marketplace— And then rips it off.

My book *Time and Temperature* is an experiment in writing while thinking. I had decided not to use my writing as a display or as a method of persuasion, but only as a tool for following, directing and critiquing my own attitudes. I put certain questions to myself. There was a bit of method to my madness, but I wouldn't call it science. It was mostly self-therapy, which eventually I culled and processed into a creative work. It has presented some challenges as a literary product in the mass media market, because it doesn't fit into any available slots and is difficult to explain. Plus, it contains some really radical messages like, "Everyone should take a nap."

Time and Temperature is dedicated to Gertrude Stein and Albert Einstein, "two minds I admire." What these two individuals, an artist and a scientist, represent to me is a rejection of programmed thought, a willingness to experience the magic of the mind without exerting utter control over it—or trying to.

I think that our inclination to clamp down on our thoughts comes from fear. Our fear response is our survival mechanism. Our level of self-awareness, so uniquely human, creates abundant opportunities to be fearful. The field of cognitive science provides knowledge that we can use to overcome outdated evolutionary programming that causes anxiety. But, it can also be used to manipulate our thinking and activate the fear response. I don't refer only to the overt fear-mongering that we have seen so much of lately. Scientific studies have demonstrated that we have a physiological response to those flickering shapes on the TV, the rapid cuts and scene changes.

Artists have long used an intuitive understanding of perceptual and cognitive functions to manipulate audience response—that's what we do. Over the centuries we've formalized our knowledge into systems which we call the rules of design. But traditionally our intent has been to express ourselves, not to dominate others. We let the audience take away what they will. We know that for any given work, not everyone will get it. Maybe, as with Gertrude Stein, very few will. But the ones who don't get it, still get something. Everyone may have their unique, personal experience of the work. The exchange between artist and audience amounts to a sort of dialogue that takes place across many small and large divides and even across time.

Contemporary design and mass communications employ a more dictatorial approach. Here the object is to make sure everyone gets the same message, right away, for the purpose of attaining very specific outcomes. The artfully designed message is delivered with scientific precision. And we do get that message, whether we are conscious of it or not, or aware of who's message it is, or what their true motives are. We could be more aware, if we were schooled in what to look for and how to critically evaluate what we find. And if we were more skilled in crafting our own messages, we'd do better at countering the propaganda.

Here is what I gained from the study of art, and what I would like everyone to gain from the study of art, regardless of whether they are or want to be artists:

I learned to really observe what I was looking at. I acquired manual dexterity. I learned about planning and problem-solving. I learned to carry a project through to completion. I was encouraged to express myself. These skills, instilled early, prepare a child for success in every endeavor and field of study, and contribute to healthy emotional development as well.

I learned to translate the three-dimensional world into a two-dimensional picture, and in doing so I learned that the eye can be fooled, and the brain can be fooled; that real things can be made to look fantastic and fantastic things can be made to look real. This awareness is essential for critical thinking.

Having been a disinterested underachiever in math and science, I learned a lot of math and a lot of science in the course of working with art supplies. Not to mention figuring out their cost and how to pay for them.

I learned about humanity, human history, psychology, culture, religion, philosophy, social movements and politics all in the context of studying art history.

When, in my thirties, I took up writing seriously, I realized that virtually all of the lessons of my visual art education applied equally to creative writing. The entire gamut of visual techniques corresponded to an array of literary techniques concerning structure, rhythm, point of view, and the like. Further, having devoted so much time to learning to see and observe, I found I had a capacity to visualize that served my writing well. Initially, all I tried to do was describe in words what I saw in my mind's eye.

But then the words went to work on me. I had already attained a level of empathy from my study of art. My art history professor in college clicked through her slides of

Paleolithic and Neolithic art and told us: "The people who made these things were the same as us." When I began to write, I discovered the ability to do more than empathize with a group in aggregate. I could put myself into the mind of a particular person. From my own experience and observation I could invent many different sorts of characters. And when I did this, I began to understand that in order for a character to work in fiction, there must be a consistency at the core that allows the reader to either believe or be surprised at his response to events. Real people also behave in character and sometimes out of character. This seems so obvious; but when it really started to sink in, and I began to write in a journal about my observations of myself and others, I found myself becoming more accepting, if not less critical, of my fellow humans.

Writing fiction helped me get an objective grip on the world. It took me out of myself. It made me the creator and ruler of a universe where I could address absolutely any topic, from any angle, with every sort of device. I could tell a fantastic story for the fun of it, and tell my own fortune in the process. Every sort of experience and emotion works its way to the surface in the writing of fiction. Interestingly, there is now research out showing that *reading* fiction increases empathy, as well.

In conclusion, the arts have been an untapped resource for the humanist community, and artists are very much in need of humanists' support. I would like to see humanists rally around art in the same way we have rallied around science. We should include a thorough study of visual art—fine, applied, theory and history—in the humanist curriculum, and lobby for its return to the public schools. We have never needed it more.

Visual literacy, and a general understanding of the perceptual and cognitive processes involved in graphic design, music, film and language, are survival skills in our technological age. An understanding of the principles and history of art provides the ammunition rational people need to identify, challenge and counter the unhelpful myths and manipulations of mass media and corporate culture. As unique, complex individuals, we naturally seek creative outlets and interpersonal connections. Here, too, we turn to the arts, not as a luxury, but as a necessary component of personal and societal health.

The Arts and Sciences together have been a winning combination for human civilization. Just as humanists have been ardent defenders of Science, so we must be strong champions for Art.

Part 1

Our Best Selves

Selected Essays from the
Humanist Society of New Mexico *Newsletter*
January 2011 – December 2012

New Year's Resolution
January 2011

My New Year's resolution for 2011 is to not be the one who's red in the face, foaming at the mouth, and incoherent with anger—unlike I was on the Monday morning after Thanksgiving, when two Evangelicals rang the bell. I lit right into them about how many times I had told "you people" not to come on the premises. "Who do you think you are, that you get to talk to me about my spirituality. . . ." The anger was making me too short of breath to speak. Meanwhile, the dog was right behind me barking sharply, and Frank, hearing the notes of alarm, came charging to our defense. In his big choral conductor voice he commanded the women to leave the property at once. They were more than happy to do so.

"What did they say to make you so mad?"

"Nothing." I felt embarrassed. "They didn't say a word. I just saw the Bible in her hands and lost it." I was feeling more stupid by the second. How could the mere arrival of those two smiling, well-groomed, diminutive women make me lose my cool like that?

This depth of feeling reflects lessons instilled deep in childhood. I wasn't very old before I learned a big word, "assimilation," for a big sin. The frightening part of assimilation was that even if you didn't want to commit such a sin, you might be compelled to choose between preserving your life or preserving your identity. This was not an academic topic in our household. One side of the family had fled the pogroms in Russia, the other had been herded into Poland's Warsaw Ghetto, where many died. Our people had not come through such hardships to this brilliant land of equality and religious freedom only to be absorbed into the dominant Christian culture.

So, you can see how having strangers show up un-invited to insert their unwelcome piety into my happy home really sets me off. I no longer practice the traditions of Judaism, but I'm hardly assimilated. If anything, my outrage at Christian proselytizing has only increased.

It used to be fun, as a kid, to see my grandmother welcome in the unsuspecting Seventh Day Adventists for a chat, and then cream them with her superior knowledge of the Old Testament. As a Jew, such visits are not threatening—I never expect the knock on the door will be the gestapo come to drag me away. But as an American, a patriot to the core by virtue of prior generations' immigrant experience, I am enraged by the *chutzpah* of someone trying to foist their religion on me.

The Buddha taught: "Do not fight in anger." A local wise man taught me this: "There are real reasons to be angry. People do wrong and hurtful things. But what are you going to do, be mad forever? Anger is a strong emotion and it makes us feel strong, but in reality it weakens us." His words have registered ever more deeply over the years.

There is only one thing now that really and truly

makes me lose it—door-to-door proselytizing. But I am resolved this year: Deep breaths, count to ten, smile.

Happy New Year, Humanists! Let's remember to be happy humanists, not angry humanists. We are indeed in a fight for a freer and fairer society, but we need not fight in anger. We can address our problems with reason and our adversaries with respect. We are our own best advertisement for our philosophy when we demonstrate how humanism allows us to be our best selves.

Just Say "Yes"
February 2011

Some call it Karma, which is the principle that when one does good deeds and acts honorably, those "positive vibes" are reflected back, and good things will come of good behavior. Some call it a Blessing, where doing good brings rewards from God in the form of a good life. Some call it The Golden Rule, wherein understanding one's own wants and needs allows one to understand others' needs. It is both logical and loving to suppose that by treating others with respect and kindness, one can expect to be treated in the same manner.

Some call it Science, as in DNA. Each one of us is encoded with such survival skills as the ability to work together and the need for approval from others in our tribe. Behaving agreeably is then a necessary reflex.

Some call it Math, in that the more one reaches out to help others, the more friends one makes; the more one's network and influence grows; the more one's reputation spreads, and the more likely that everyone, in turn, will be helped by this network.

You could call it Common Sense. When one participates constructively and generously in a community, all our lives are enriched. We are supported personally by the relationships we build, and in the process we build a stronger, better-functioning society.

Whatever you call it, humans are eager to please and to be praised by each other. We like the word Yes. Yes, I will help you. Yes, I approve of what you are doing. Yes, you are valued. Yes, you can count on me. What is this mechanism that, when it's working right, causes human beings to come together, to say Yes, and to create a whole that is greater than the sum of its parts?

HSNM is a laboratory. Here we explore the possibilities for a humanistic society. Can we live by our principles and balance personal freedom with social responsibility? Can we say Yes and feel rewarded by what is asked of us? What can we accomplish together? How much might we each grow personally by giving a little extra energy to help reach the group's goals?

Since I said Yes to HSNM, I have worked very hard at it and felt very good. What is this good stuff? Has my Karma improved? Maybe God is blessing me. Reason and reflection tell me that all of this good stuff actually comes from all of you. Having more bright, caring, thoughtful, open-minded people in my life has been good for me. I recommend it. When the opportunity to pitch in for a worthy cause comes around, just say Yes.

Am Honored to Inscribe
March 2011

In 1994 I attended a talk by Henry Roth, author of *Call It Sleep*. This intense novel of immigrant Jewish life in the U.S. was published in 1934, when Roth was 28 years old. The book received critical acclaim, but then it languished for decades until its release in paperback in 1964, when a front-page review in *The New York Times Book Review* launched it to bestseller status. Time passed, thirty more years, and still Roth did not publish another novel.

The occasion for Roth's re-entry into public life was the publication, at last, of a new novel, *Mercy of a Rude Stream*. My own project at the time was a collection titled *Ancestral Notes*, research for which had led me to *Call It Sleep*. I wrote to Roth, who now lived in Albuquerque, asking if he would read my manuscript. He replied that he needed all of his energy to complete his own work. The point was driven home when I joined the standing-room-only crowd at Temple Albert to see the frail 88-year-old.

Roth was gratified, but not complacent. He had three more volumes to complete, he announced, and intended to do so. But we could feel the doubt that hovered over this ambitious project. In fact, he only lived one year longer, leaving his editors to hammer out the final volumes from the 2,000 pages he had written.

What did Roth have to say about his literary career? About his legendary writer's block? About the thirty years during which this new work had gestated? I will never forget the substance of his message, though after all this time I must paraphrase: "What I am most proud of about this book, which was not true of 'Call It Sleep,' is that it was written by a good man."

He went on to talk about the callow youth who had penned that astonishing first novel. That man was not anyone the elder Roth would care to claim or know. But in all the years which had passed since, years in which he'd lived a mundane life of husband, father, laborer and teacher, he had accomplished something much more significant: he had become a *mensch*. And he reported that he stood before us on that day as a decent human being, and this was his measure of success.

After the talk I stood in line to get Roth's autograph on my copy of *Call It Sleep*. He remembered our correspondence, and wrote on the dedication page: "For Zelda Leah Gatuskin / I anticipate the work will be noteworthy / Am honored to inscribe / Henry Roth"

Others inspired me during this time. Regina Turner, HSNM's guest speaker for March, was bringing the International Anne Frank Exhibit to New Mexico through the NM Human Rights Projects. I clipped the articles and re-read the Anne Frank autobiography, as I dug deeper and deeper into my family roots and my own consciousness. Regina herself became a role model and friend. I participated in a small way in the exhibit and surrounding activities, but my focus was still mostly on myself, my book and my writing career.

It's easy to fixate on specific projects and goals. Passion and ego drive us along. Accomplishments and credits accumulate. Sometimes we achieve brilliance; occasionally the world notices. But fundamentally there is only one task before us that is necessary, if we are to live in a humane society, and that is to become decent human beings—preferably before our energy is spent.

Dogs and Cats
April 2011

There is a new addition to our household—a spunky terrier mutt named Beau. I took Beau off Janet J's hands in January. He was stirring up trouble with the other seven dogs (her own and rescues). Once I had plucked Beau out of the pack of seven squabbling dachshunds, Janet's life improved immediately. Our household, on the other hand, went into an uproar—two humans not so well disciplined ourselves, two cats terrorized by this frisky little guy not much bigger than they, and Millie—the only one who took things in stride. Millie is also a terrier mutt, but twice Beau's size. She proudly demonstrated how to be a "good dog."

Beau arrived at likely his fifth home in as many years with some understandable anxieties and bad behaviors that spring from fear. He got into more trouble out of excess energy and enthusiasm. We were on his case constantly: No barking, no whining, no scratching, NO CAT, no taking Millie's toy, no getting underfoot, no begging in the kitchen. . . .

Scientific and anecdotal evidence indicates that dogs are able to acquire extensive vocabularies, but there is a limit. After a couple of weeks I found myself, in exasperation, condensing my commands to a mere two: "Chill out!" and "Shape up!" It occurred to me that I also live my life between these two directives.

Chill out. Don't jump on every bandwagon, don't fret and obsess, don't make so much work for yourself and others, don't allow emotion or ambition to stir up undue stress and anxiety. Cool it with self-righteousness and self-importance. At the other extreme of the pendulum: Shape up. Get on with it, stop procrastinating, don't skip any steps, try harder, live by your principles and ideals. If it's worth doing, it's worth doing right.

How exhausting even to write this! I've given up expecting that my inner pendulum might come to rest lightly in the middle, balanced between overdoing and underachieving. I can only try to make its arc less extreme, its movement more gentle, and to be honest and aware when it comes to my personal foibles, fears and fantasies.

Eight weeks in, Beau and the big cat (they are nearly the same size) have touched noses and made friends. The little cat is still frightened by Beau's overtures, though he's done an admirable job of toning down his doggy come-on. We don't try to protect her anymore, or keep the two separated for safety—the displays are becoming more like play and keep us laughing.

Humans, like dogs and cats, can be conditioned to accept new situations and to behave contrary to our natural instincts. In principle the methods are not much different than a bop on the nose with a rolled up newspaper, but in practice they have become highly sophisticated and costly, to the point that we should suspect the motives of those footing the bill.

Our April speaker has been a leader in critiquing mass media and challenging its unhealthy influences on society. Who is trying to manipulate us and why? Bob McCannon of the Action Coalition for Media Education will pull aside the curtain to reveal the devices of our contemporary media wizards.

Humanism is not an exercise in finding a position and then standing stubbornly on it. It is a sometimes slow, sometimes lively dance on a shifting stage. Occasionally we may find ourselves climbing the walls or in the doghouse. What matters is that we have the capacity and the will to learn new tricks.

And if that doesn't get you to our next meeting, how about a cookie?

Virtue and Honor
May 2011

An afternoon or evening in the company of a creative work can be more nourishing than a seven-course meal, more refreshing than a good night's sleep. This was certainly true in the case of *La Traviata*, recently performed at the KiMo Theater—a true masterwork beautifully produced by Albuquerque's own Opera Southwest. The leading roles were played by visiting professionals, and guest conductor Francesco Milioto did a masterful job of meshing them with an orchestra and chorus of local musicians. The show provided both balm for the soul and food for thought. Opera can certainly be an acquired taste, and it helps to know the libretto, but the lyricism of Verdi transcends its time, place and language. You could close your eyes and love this opera without knowing anything about it.

Some of us have trouble getting past the pathetic plots which characterize opera in general. This tragedy, like all opera tragedies, hinges on the virtue—or lack thereof—of its women characters. Violetta, a courtesan (such a word!) falls in love with Alfredo, a young man of esteemed lineage, but is persuaded to end the relationship by his father (Germont) for the sake of his sister, a chaste young thing betrothed to a nobleman. If the family name is besmirched by the son's liaison, it will ruin the daughter's chance for this marriage—

leading one to ask: What kind of jerk is the father, or for that matter the fiance? God is invoked frequently, with apparent sincerity, by one and all. But the words are sometimes dripping with irony, such as Violetta's adamant, "God forgives but man does not."

Later, Violetta sings, "Religion is a great comfort to those who suffer." At the performance I attended, a good half of the audience tittered at this line. I wondered if our modern sensibilities caused us to read into this a modern disconnect between genuine grace and mere palliative, until I studied the program notes and learned that the opera is based on a novel by that clever cynic, Alexandre Dumas. Indeed, it is the father who must suffer remorse and atone, not the so-called fallen woman, whose dignity and virtue were apparent at every turn. Germont sends Alfredo back to Violetta, and himself offers her fatherly love and blessings whilst she dies of tuberculosis. Well, she has to die. Dumas was no dummy. Mores of the time, not to mention theatrical convention, demanded nothing less.

Much as I enjoyed the music, staging and performances of *La Traviata*, I came away thinking that for all the lip service paid to protecting women's virtue and honor, there is little honor actually paid to women—no more now than ever—and hardly anything like fatherly love in the general sense. Women as a class continue to be treated callously and disrespectfully in much of the world including here at home. That said, let's not forget that Violetta is the one consistently admirable character in the story. She was played by diva Shana Blake Hill, who stole the show with her vibrant and virtuostic performance—a real-life super-hero of song, and a role model for free and accomplished womanhood.

In the months to come we will consider women's issues and the needs of other undervalued segments of society, because a humanistic world view respects and supports all of the players on life's stage.

Believe It or Not
June 2011

I've noticed that my conversations with prospective HSNM members must always contain a "belief" segment. There is concern for what humanists might and might not believe, and if the interested party properly aligns with our perceived or assumed doctrine.

Humanism is often equated with Atheism or an anti-religion posture, but our use of the term Naturalism may sometimes be construed as placing us on the opposite end of the spectrum among nature worshipers, pantheists and various metaphysical orders. What generally puts everyone at ease and allows conversation to shift away from potential points of conflict to broad points of agreement, is when I blurt out: "I don't care what anyone believes or doesn't believe, and I don't think it's anyone's business what I believe."

I go on to talk about the ideal of a secular society, in which we are all free to follow and express the belief or philosophy of our choice yet prohibited from imposing our ways on others. This is where heads start to nod in agreement.

Humanist philosophy separates ethics from beliefs, and places responsibility for human behavior squarely on the shoulders of humanity, regardless of its members' personal spiritual feelings. The phrase "humanist philosophy" itself implies that we are able to debate approaches to living and social structure without reference to supernatural elements. I would even argue that the insertion of belief/disbelief into the mix hinders fruitful discussion.

How can I argue with anyone's beliefs? How can I disprove anyone's disbelief? Of more concern to me personally: How can I possibly properly articulate my own beliefs? My beliefs are a moving target, I find, and defy my efforts to pin them down. I've been writing for many years. I have written around and around the questions of what I think and feel and believe, and the overall state of my consciousness at any given time. In a short poem or a 400-page novel, I can come close to conveying, to my own satisfaction, my take on life and the world I live in. I am satisfied with those forms because they are holistic, they encircle and approach the ideas from multiple perspectives.

Linear arguments do not help me get to my deepest-held beliefs. I can write a sentence with precision from beginning to end concerning what I believe, but the moment I add that period, I discover that the words do not ring true. They are a two-dimensional representation of a multi-dimensional phenomenon. I'm happier when

47

I let myself be than when I make myself express a firm, unyielding belief.

I want to work for and live in a secular society where belief is a private matter, and what we talk about publicly is respect. If you as a person respect me as a person, then it doesn't matter how we label ourselves. We can focus on our working relationship. Who cares what either of us believes, as long as we are pulling together to make our world better and modeling compassionate, constructive, ethical behavior?

Societies have always had ways of dealing with people who behave badly. Right now we have some extremely bad players in society who wrap themselves in the mantles of religious, nationalistic or economic dogma. The torrent of rhetoric about "believing in" one thing or another deflects scrutiny and criticism of their actual behavior. I think we're all getting sick of it. It's time to get away from distracting "belief" debates and engage in substantive discussions—leading to action—about fairness, freedom and respect.

It's Time to Get Serious About the Universal Declaration of Human Rights
July 2011

How much do you know about the Universal Declaration of Human Rights? Eleanor Roosevelt chaired the United Nations committee that drafted the UDHR, which was adopted by the United Nations on December 10, 1948. The United States was a signatory nation, but in the ensuing years we have not walked the talk. Our country has assiduously avoided ratifying several international legal treaties that together constitute an International Bill of Rights to give the weight of law to the thirty human rights enshrined in the Declaration.

Think about the highly politicized issues dividing our country today, and how differently we would have to approach them if we truly embraced the meaning of this Declaration. We could stop arguing about who should be entitled to what and start figuring out how to guarantee everyone the fundamental security and dignity that civilized, compassionate human beings recognize to be the birthright of all.

If you are feeling overwhelmed by the number and severity of problems facing our country and the world at this moment, look at the foundation that has been laid for us by others who lived in hard times. Extraordinary work has been done. It is a fitting task for our humanist societies to carry the mission forward. Let's consider what we can do to educate the public about Universal Human Rights, and bring the weight of public opinion to bear on our leaders to put deeds to words.

[The complete text of the Universal Declaration of Human Rights is included as an Appendix to this book, as taken from the web site of the Office of the United Nations High Commissioner for Human Rights at ohchr.org. This text is in the public domain, and the web site provides a printable version for download. May I suggest: Make copies to share with friends and associates; add the UDHR link to your signature line; introduce the UDHR as a topic of discussion in your spiritual, philosophical or political meetings. Not only does the document bring up moral and practical issues worthy of serious discussion, it encourages us to plunge into history and remember the context in which it was composed. In the aftermath of two massive wars fought within a mere half-century, representatives from around the world came together in good faith to draft a social contract for humanity calling for world peace, universal freedom and secure living conditions for all. It is up to us to promote and pursue their vision.]

Can't We Just Evolve Already?
April 2012

Do you ever find yourself wishing that *Homo sapiens* would hurry up and evolve already?

Clearly it is the unique quality of the human mind that has given us the evolutionary edge so far. Language, self-awareness, science, imagination—other species possess intelligence, but none has been able, individually or collectively, to organize theirs in the way that humans have made routine for the past fifty thousand years or more. While the common notion that we only ever use about ten percent of our brains has been soundly de-bunked, there is evidence that, regardless of how many cylinders are firing, we're dumber in groups. (With the exception of groups of humanists, of course—and by the way, the topic for our next Discussion Meeting will be "Snobbery, Elitism and Humanism.")

Humans can work together effectively to build just about anything, fight wars, harvest crops and process food; but getting together intellectually is more problematic. New ideas are most often met with some combination of derision and fear. Small groups of curious, broad-minded individuals push forward along-side or close behind a "genius"—a Plato, daVinci, Newton, Beethoven, Darwin, Jefferson, Picasso—and, in direct proportion to their progress, a great force of reactionary hysterics pulls back to center, to the status quo, and may even try to go backwards. We are seeing that backlash acted out today in multiple arenas.

In groups, we approach problems from the assumption that they exist independently of ourselves, and that solutions will come through manipulating and "fixing" something "out there," in the same way we might adjust the temperature of the oven or put air in a tire. But social order problems do not arise from external forces so much as from the internal makeup of the species attempting to organize. To quote Walt Kelly's *Pogo*, "We have met the enemy and he is us."

Look around at the problems plaguing our communities, nations and humanity itself. Does it seem like every attempt at a solution digs us in deeper? Why is that? Could it be a failure of imagination, of compassion, of some inherent but underdeveloped capacity of consciousness?

Can we make the next evolutionary leap without going over the cliff and taking a significant portion of nature as we know it with us? I think we can, but like all species that must adapt to new conditions or face extinction, we will need to diversify our gene pool, by which I mean our gene pool of ideas—our "meme pool" (the word "meme" itself being an example of how concepts evolve). What game-changing ideas have we missed out on, over the course of the last few millennia, by marginalizing the voices of everyone who is not a white, male, Judeo-Christian landowner from the Western world? (Note that all of the trailblazers listed above do fall into that elite category.) Perceived in this light, extending equal rights, opportunities and respect to all people, everywhere, is not just a matter of being fair to them, it's a question of survival for all.

Nature Is Inescapable
May 2012

Spring is quickly moving into summer, and the irrigation ditch where we take our daily walks affords many opportunities to observe nature, tamed and untamed and all stages in between. I'm impressed by how plant and animal life have adapted to changing conditions over the years. I remember when the water came down the ditch twice a week; then it was limited to once a week; and for the past several years, we only get water every other week. And yet, there is a pair of ducks that still makes our ditch their part-time home. Wherever they were all winter, and wherever they go in the off weeks, they continue to appear every spring with the first flow of water. They can be found paddling about happily when the water is high, or flying overhead from one lingering puddle to the next as the water drains away.

Ducks in the desert—raising babies, no less—hardly troubled by the people and dogs walking or trotting along beside them; bravely co-existing with predatory hawks, roadrunners, tame and feral cats, and who-knows-what-all that comes out at night.

Nature is not only resilient, it's relentless. Mustard weeds have grown waist-high already in the bone-dry back alley. The ants' nests are swarming back to life. Wherever a small rock casts a small shadow in which a drop of moisture can linger, a tiny tumbleweed sprouts. Even more impressive, given my decidedly not-green thumb, the intentional plantings have mostly survived and in some cases thrived.

My biggest success has been with the wisteria in front of my studio, positioned to grow for shade and color over the wrought iron that protects the big, south-facing window. Poor thing couldn't even shade itself at first. For several summers we had to put a sort of tent over it in the hottest months. But this spring I am sitting in the dappled light of a healthy vine that drips with lush purple blooms. Yes, I had a hand in its success, but still, I was only giving an assist to nature to do what it does anyway.

And that's my point. That's all we're ever doing. We are in nature, part of nature, working with nature. Our own minds are an ecosystem of sorts. Are we going to let them be paved over, or can we allow a little space there for something to grow? Thoughts and emotions are part of our organic nature. Perception, consciousness, creativity, curiosity, analysis, learning—these are natural processes that are not readily suppressed. Surely if they could be quieted, they would be by now, given the immense exertions throughout history of power-greedy control freaks and their punishing institutions.

And what of the future? We have in our collective imagination unpleasant images of humanity becoming programed, robotic, or actually increasingly inorganic, while the "State" manages a homogeneous, mechanized society with dictatorial dispassion. Some might see certain aspects of contemporary culture as evidence that we are already well down that path.

What role can we play as humanists to prevent the nightmare from coming true? Shall we respond with a counter set of maneuvers designed to impose the social format we prefer on those we consider less enlightened or less well-intentioned? I would rather we simply be that drop of water, that spot of shade, that crack in the pavement in which minds and hearts may naturally grow—naturally good, strong and beautiful—thus creating more and more fertile soil where all can thrive.

EHFAR
September 2012

"Everything happens for a reason." How often have you heard that one? I think it is time to address this ubiquitous, mostly mindless utterance head-on.

Of course everything happens for a reason, just not in the way the saying is generally intended. Most often, someone will make this observation in reference to a negative or seemingly negative occurrence resulting in something positive that followed or will surely follow: "I didn't get the job," but, "Everything happens for a reason"—maybe there will be a better job down the road. "I didn't win the tournament," but, EHFAR, I've discovered a weakness that I can work on so I can win in the future. "My family suffered a devastating loss," (these are the ones that truly disturb me) but—EHFAR—we have been brought closer together and learned valuable lessons.

For some time now, my response to EHFAR has been: "Well, everything happens, and because we have the minds that we have, we give it a reason." Lately though, I'm tempted to be more sharp: "You bet that happened for a reason...." You didn't get the job because your skills/connections/effort weren't as good as someone else's. You didn't win the game because the opposing player or team had practiced more, was stronger or simply luckier when it mattered. The family tragedy occurred in the manner of all events—one thing leads to another through some combination of intended and unintended actions and the results of those actions unscrolling in logical sequence. The laws of nature do not make exception. They amount to reasons, as in causes, that dictate a chain of events and their outcome.

As for the future—what transpires following the incident to which we feel compelled to ascribe "reason," in the sense that some higher power or our destiny must have intended or required that result—it is our own consciousness and free will that allow us to create meaning and positive attitudes and actions going forward. EHFAR is the rationalization humans use to make lemonade out of lemons. With this in mind, I am working on a new response to EHFAR:

"If you mean there were causes and circumstances that resulted in those unfortunate events, then I agree with you. Whether this will have meaning and usefulness for you in the future is your choice, and I'm glad you have chosen to deal with the situation constructively rather than surrender to despair."

EHFAR isn't really very comforting when the "reason" part refers to the supposed intentions of a supernatural force. A god that prefers to heap on suffering versus gently instilling enlightenment (one would think a hands-on, all-powerful, all-loving being could do that) deserves the wrath of Job, not an appreciative "EHFAR."

It is not necessary to let EHFAR and other stock platitudes go by unanswered. We can rebut them or state our own view in a way that is challenging but still respectful and kind. In doing so we may find that the old saw was spoken by rote, and the speaker is not uttering a deeply-held conviction but repeating words barely considered. You could be jump-starting someone's dormant critical thinking skills and liberating them from the trap of fatalism. Or not. But if you get flak for speaking your mind about EHFAR, you can turn it back on itself and reply, "If everything happens for a reason, then this conversation is happening for a reason too. Maybe you should think about it!"

Save Us from the Soul-Savers
November 2012

Katherine Stewart recently sent me a copy of her book *The Good News Club* (PublicAffairs, 2012). I read it with alarm. It is a well researched and engagingly written account of a strategic, determined effort to insert one particular religious view into public schools, and it specifically targets the lower grades. The well-funded Child Evangelism Fellowship (CEF) has a sort of soul-saving franchise known as The Good News Club, which local churches are urged to sponsor. The package comes with training, branding, and a portfolio of legal strategies for allowing activities on public property under free speech rights that had once been forbidden on church/state-separation grounds.

It boils down to this: If a church club or Bible Study group can use school property when school is not in session in the same way secular clubs may; and if impressionable children happen to construe an after-school religious "class" to bear the same authority as the lessons taught during school hours; and if the children then repeat to their peers something they learned from the church group *during* their school classes—well, they are only exercising their right to free speech, and that should be (and has been judged to be) permissible.

Are you turning purple yet? There is so much wrong here, I'll touch on only two aspects that trouble me—and they are not the obvious constitutional issues:

My first concern is with the well-meaning, devout adults who are drawn into these Good News Club start-ups that inevitably split their communities (hence the arsenal of legal strategies). They are not blind to the strife they cause, or unfeeling toward those neighbors, teachers and school officials who oppose them (and do sometimes win). But they have surrendered their personal authority and common sense to a Higher Power whose earthly intermediaries have a ready answer for every twinge of conscience. "God will take care of it," troubled trainees are told. And so the answer to Katherine's hard questions is, "God will take care of it."

What a cop-out. Of course people have the right to their religion and the right to believe and voice such assertions, but how sad for them personally to forgo the use of their (God-given?) capacities for empathy and reason. Clearly CEF's mind-molding is not limited to the children.

Which brings me to my second point. When are we going to liberate our children? When do we acknowledge that children deserve to be given the truth, as best we can figure it, so that they can grow up to grapple with reality?

The objective of child-rearing is to produce free, functional, creative, confident, caring, rational adults who are capable of surviving in a changing world, and eager to explore their full potential. That is the humanist view. Children are not chips to be pre-programmed with fears, guilt, insecurity and a weird combination of self-loathing and entitled superiority. "Our children are our future," we say (as though that weren't obvious), but we raise them to be slaves to the past or, worse, slaves to some authoritarian agenda of the day.

One is tempted to want to counter The Good News Club mission with a project to organize kids into unions to help them protect their own interests, or a movement to win children their suffrage. (If they are entitled to "free speech," why not an actual say in their own lives?) But wouldn't it be enough to simply let kids be themselves, and find themselves, while providing them with a fact-based, fun-filled, thorough education?

Changing Cottonwood Against Cloudless Sky
December 2012

We sure had a glorious autumn here while the East suffered the ravages of Hurricane Sandy. The news of the storm and its aftermath felt surreal from the vantage point of our blue skies and sunshine.

As we enjoyed a reprieve from the coming of winter, I wondered where summer had gone, and spring before that. It seemed like I had spent the year inside my computer, churning out streams of correspondence, lists, forms, code and pixels. My 2012 memories were stitched together from trips I'd made away from home: New Orleans in June, Delaware in July, Seattle in September. In between, brilliant New Mexico went by outside my window—but where was I? I decided not to let fall get away from me.

There is a spot in our backyard that provides a very good view of a large, hearty cottonwood tree. From this distance and angle I can see the entirety of its great, cloud-shaped canopy framed against the sky. For about a week I brought out a chair in the warmth of the day and just sat. The tree had progressed from sporting subtle dabs of gold to an all-out yellow-orange coif that literally glowed against the pure blue of the sky.

Each day I rested my eyes on the composition of

Changing Cottonwood Against Cloudless Sky and felt warm and content and, yes, reverent. It was a kind of meditation. My thoughts went here and there and I did not try to hold on to them. Naturally I was thinking of the places I had lived and traveled on the East Coast, and the misery many were enduring in the cold and wet, in contrast to my present comfort. But what came to mind most often was a scene from my time in Boston so many years ago:

I'd completed my freshman year at Emerson College, taken an apartment with a girlfriend, and was exploring the possibility of switching to one of the nearby art schools. To this end, I got a job at an art supply store and enrolled in several studio courses that I could attend at night. It was the fall semester. I remember walking to the subway stop after dark in the bustle and sparkle of city streets, riding in the unnatural illumination of the train and looking out at the alternating dark-light, dark-light of tunnels and platforms. Arriving in a somewhat darker and less busy neighborhood, I'd scoot around the corner to a big building and descend to a basement room in the Massachusetts College of Art.

There in the basement classroom, a young assistant professor compelled us to rule our art paper with pale pencil grids to be filled in with gouache (opaque water color), which we were learning to mix with scientific precision into hues, shades and tints. Our textbook was Johannes Itten's *The Elements of Color*, and we followed along by attempting to recreate the complementary and contrasting abutments of colored squares presented therein. I learned much about how colors are perceived differently based on their proximity to other colors. But, sitting in my backyard watching a cottonwood tree change color, it occurred to me that not a thing had gone on in that classroom, or in the damp, glittering commutes there and home again, or within the nondescript walk-up where I dabbed-in my homework grids, that came close to conveying the qualities of color provided by this common New Mexico sight—golden leaves against blue sky.

Knowing the science behind the colors of nature does not make them less beautiful. Understanding the reason we perceive certain combinations of visual elements as especially pleasing or striking does not alter those immediate emotional reactions. Being convinced that all of nature—including us—is interconnected and the result of consistent, predictable processes does not make it less awesome.

Mainly, though, I just want to share the blue sky feeling with you to carry us through the cold months. Happy HumanLight, everyone.

[HumanLight was founded as a humanist holiday by the New Jersey Humanist Network, and first observed by that group on December 23, 2001. It provides opportunity for the non-religious to join in the celebratory and charitable spirit of the winter season.]

Part 2

Let's Talk About Shoulders

Selected Essays from
"The Tree" blog
October 2012 – April 2013

Repeat After Me: ERA
October 27, 2012

Here we go again. Another right wing, Christian fundie politician has said something revoltingly offensive about women and we are tremendously exercised over it. We find the words so insulting, we can't repeat them enough. "A child conceived by rape is god's will." (I will not be offering a capital "g" to that god, you can be sure.) "Legitimate rape." "A rape victim can't get pregnant." "Slut slut slut slut."

Sisters, don't you feel like we are being dragged through the mud even by those who are ostensibly defending us? These are hurtful words in any context, especially to victims of sexual violence and targets of misogynist attacks. I think we should stop rising to the bait of a media that loves drama, conflict and sensationalism, and routinely exploits for profit all of the ugliest scenarios that have come up in the context of unwanted pregnancy. The media is no help here. They just like saying the word "rape." There is a practical solution to attacks on women's rights and we call it the ERA, which stands for Equal Rights Amendment. When was the last time you heard anyone, from any side of the political spectrum, say "ERA" over the airwaves?

The Equal Rights Amendment states: "Equality of

rights under the law shall not be denied or abridged by the United States or by any state on account of sex." It was passed by Congress in 1972, but fell three states short of the 38 states needed for full ratification under the U.S. Constitution. If the equal rights of women were enshrined in the Constitution, no municipality could legally restrict our right to access health care and make our own health care decisions, or impose any special rules on females that are not imposed on males.

Males have the right to birth control; males are not challenged when they seek insurance coverage for counseling, preventative care and treatment with respect to reproductive and sexual health. They have health issues that women don't have, but we don't begrudge them the cost of their medical care, or try to oversee the decisions they make for themselves. We need to resist on the local level whenever our rights are threatened, but let's not fall prey to divide-and-conquer "states' rights" strategies. We must have an overarching campaign to pass the ERA so that once and for all the women of this country will have equal status to men.

Read about the Equal Rights Amendment, tell your friends about it, write to your favorite pundits about it, call in to your radio shows about it, blog about it, get a bumper sticker, join or form a local group to show your congressional representatives that constituents want to move the ERA forward. Channel your outrage into action. Repeat after me: ERA!

[Visit equalrightsamendment.org for more ERA info.]

Let's Talk About Shoulders
October 31, 2012

Since we're all glued to the news during this election season, I'll write about a TV trend that's been on my mind for a while. You may have noticed this as well:

There are many more women behind the anchor desks and in front of the green screens than there used to be. In some cases, you get the feeling that producers have gone out of their way to keep an equal gender balance. The host brings in two guest commentators, one male and one female. They speak with equal facility and authority, and are treated with equal respect. But they look very different—from each other. In terms of, say, a cocktail party, the look is traditional: The man is in a suit and tie and the woman is in a bright, tight, sleeveless dress. I am starting to see more of the male commentators appear without a tie; just yesterday I saw a fellow in a preppy v-neck sweater instead of a suit jacket. Occasionally you see a man with his shirt sleeves rolled up. But I have yet to see any male newscaster or pundit appear with his shoulders bared.

So I've been paying close attention, and I find myself wishing that more women broadcasters would cover those shoulders and resist the subtle (or maybe not so subtle) pressure to do double duty as commentator and set decoration. These bright, beautiful women are no less so in sleeves. Alternatively, they can ask their male

69

counterparts to show some arm, neck and, yes, even (be still my heart) those manly shoulders.

I hope that once you have constructed that mental image for yourself—of both the man and the woman sitting there in sleeveless tops (or how about the man sleeveless and the woman in a blazer?)—you will understand why this matters, even though it's obnoxious. Human attire has always conveyed important social messages about one's function and status. Today's uniforms are less uniform than in times past but, if anything, this has put more pressure on professional women to doll themselves up.

Look closely at women broadcasters. Who is showing arms and who is not, who is sitting behind a desk and who is sitting with her legs exposed, who is standing with her entire body and outfit on display? Here, just among the women, you will find a pecking order of authority and seriousness. I bring this up because I think this is one aspect of equalizing the professional playing field that is in our own hands—and arms and shoulders.

Why "War on Women" Is a Misnomer
November 2, 2012

There is no gentle way to say this: Women are the slaves of the world. What nature dictates—that we bear and care for the offspring of the species—patriarchal society has elaborated and enshrined. For many centuries in most societies, the woman's place has been in the home performing the unpaid work on which all wealth is founded. Pick any era and think about the economics of the time. Whether based on conquest of new lands and other nations' treasure, on invention-manufacture-sales, on science-education-communications or on speculation and sophisticated abstractions of trade, expansion of community resources could not occur in the absence of day-to-day caretaking of food, clothing and shelter. A baseline of physical security must be achieved before one can turn attention to more ambitious goals.

Our patriarchs, desiring to claim the life of the mind exclusively for themselves, foisted on our matriarchs the exclusive burden of caring not only for their babies, but also children and grown-up men, plus the aged and infirm, as well as the home and grounds and livestock. All of this was women's work—right up to the point that the operation became large enough to require machinery or more "hands" than the mother and her children (another source of unpaid labor) could provide. Until very recently, women have been generally uneducated and barred from work outside the home. The rationalizations for this are identical to those offered by apologists for black slavery prior to the Civil War: Women/blacks were not bright enough to gain from formal schooling, not emotionally fit to deal with the complexities of the world beyond their doorsteps, in need of ongoing correction and protection. And they *were* paid—the "pay" being the protection itself, of course. The women/slaves weren't working for free, but earning their keep.

Get it? Women who are considered to have no intrinsic value to society beyond their bodies and their labor are *kept*—like pets or beasts of burden. (Some have it easier than others.) Fathers give their daughters over to the keeping of husbands, labor is transferred from one household to another. In the best circumstance, the wife can be assured of a provider and protector to the end of her days. She doesn't *need* to work for pay, and of course she doesn't need to earn as much as those male "providers" when she does work outside the home.

Sex on demand has also been part of the marital job description for women. Is it any wonder that men who consider themselves the boss in the bedroom also consider themselves the boss of the female body and entitled to make all reproductive decisions?

It sure feels like an assault to some of us, but don't call it a war on women. We are dealing with people who fervently or conveniently or unthinkingly believe that God is the Father, His representatives to humankind are Males, and Women are the Males' handmaidens, equally blessed by God with a particular, precious role to play in the divine hierarchy. How dare we accuse these faithful of making war on the very creatures they have been charged with protecting!

Masters do not make war on their slaves. There are rebellions and reprisals, but outright war is reserved for the worthy foe, one considered to be in a position of strength. The Civil War was a war between the states to see whose interpretation of the Constitution would shape the future of our republic; it was not a war between empowered whites and disempowered blacks. Today's "war on women" is very much the same; it is a battle between and within branches of government over who will define and defend the "rights" of those who are presently oppressed.

"War on women" has been useful for rallying women's rights supporters and activists, but I don't think it's accurate. If this is a war, then it's the longest war in history. Yet women are not competing with men for a "share" of freedom as if it were a limited resource with only so much to go around; and there is nothing we possess that we have not willingly contributed to humanity in the insoluble partnership that naturally exists between males and females. For there to be a war, there has to be a foe, and we are not the foe. No, "war" is too grand a word for this reactionary backlash to anything that challenges the status quo male dominance.

So, what would I call it? Desperation. The panic of the male ruling class at the prospect of sharing power. It's never a pretty sight, and these have been troubling times, but I always count it as progress when unseen machinations are finally revealed. Housekeepers of both genders know that you need to get a good look at the problem in order to clean it up. Now that we have this mess exposed to the light of day, let's name it for what it is—patriarchy on parade.

Our "founding fathers" did not give women equal status in the Constitution. The pronoun "she" does not appear in that document. Amendments XIII, XIV and XV, which abolish slavery and grant civil rights and voting rights to blacks, do not explicitly pertain to women, and in fact intentionally exclude reference to women. So there's no need for anyone to make war on us, and we are in no position to make war on men. With female representation in Congress at a mere 17 percent, women in this country are still stuck with only one recourse, which is to plead for our male overlords to finally pass the ERA and write us into the Constitution. And that does make me fighting mad.

Lrch Frwrd
November 11, 2012

I wish the media would not appropriate perfectly good words for their slogans. First of all, we need those words, and do not want immediate mental associations to some corporate identity. I know that this is exactly the reason the phrases are chosen, but hear me out, because— Second of all, words that make sense in a sentence where they serve a necessary descriptive or instructive purpose are dumb in isolation.

Take MSNBC's "lean forward." That turned me off immediately. I could just imagine the intense brainstorming session that was held around that one: How do we say we're progressive without *saying* "progressive"? It needs to have *action*, to make people feel *active*. Yeah, and *emphatic*, like it's in *italics*. Right, right—and what do italics do? They lean forward— *Lean forward!* Perfect! It's got visual meaning, political meaning, and marketing meaning—we want folks to be so into MSNBC, they *lean forward* when they watch!

I don't know. "Lean forward" brings to mind a figure who is somewhat unbalanced, possibly ready to trip or tip over; or someone pushing against a hard wind; or someone who's fixin' to get a swat on the nose—virtual or literal—for sticking it where it doesn't belong. Some of us politically progressive types, when confronted with something new and different, would still rather pause at a safe distance and poke it with a stick before we lean forward. In folk dancing, the "lean" as a dance step is never done exclusively in one direction. It's dancing, after all, and not falling over. A big lean in one direction is followed nicely by a lean in the other direction. Or you might have a quick lean-lean and then settle back to center.

We have the word "lean" suggesting imbalance, and then we have the word "forward," highly useful but now unfortunately shaded by the insidious slogan. So that when President Obama says "Forward!" it sounds like he's a shill for the progressive network that cheers him on. It also sounds vaguely military, like "Onward!" Now, even an innocent email from our re-elected Senator Udall labeled "Going Forward" feels a little sinister. You too, Tom? But that's what we're doing— pushing on, planning for the future—going "forward." I like the word forward, but not as much as I used to.

Lean forward is what we do when we don't want to get something on ourselves, like when we have to spit, or when we're eating a slice of greasy pizza. I might lean forward if I can't hear you; I could lean forward to smell a rose and avoid the thorns.

While I enjoy MSNBC and put on Rachel and Lawrence almost every night, I don't sit there leaning forward to catch every word—I'm usually doing things around the house or at the computer. When I do actually watch, that "lean forward" campaign with those earnest cameos by the star commentators drives me nuts. You'd think *they* were the ones running for office, while "lean forward" scrolls along the top of the screen, more of a stage direction than slogan.

"Lean forward" seems obviously intended to convey "left-leaning." That's kind of a funny counterpoint to Fox News labeling themselves "fair and balanced" when they clearly tilt way to the right. Note that the phrase "fair and balanced" is ruined too; now we use it facetiously with air quotes. Given our obsession with making media devices smaller and messages shorter, I suppose we can look ~~forward~~ (darn!) *ahead* to even more cryptic branding, at which point the words the rest of us need to communicate will be safe. Instead of "fair and balanced" and "lean forward" the partisan networks can just use Xs and Os, which we can interpret in the way that best fits our world view, which is what we do anyway.

Mirror Mirror
November 13, 2012

"You've come a long way, baby!" Remember that one? By 1968 women had come so far that Madison Avenue designed a cigarette just for us. Since then, they have taken us on quite a merry romp in the "updating" of womanhood. In TV and movies, we have seen our roles transformed. Where once the female role was to provide utilitarian set decoration—a buxom girl with steno pad off in the corner, a nurse poised prettily two paces behind the wealthy male patient or distinguished doctor—women characters began to take center stage in boardrooms, courtrooms and, of course, bedrooms. Women could now be initiators in sexual encounters, a situation apparently both exciting and unnerving for the mostly male minds concocting these plots, as suggested by the easy transformation of female sexual aggressor to female maniacal murderer or tough-girl avenger.

Hollywood had it all figured out: If a good-looking woman looked good on the periphery of the action, imagine how she'd look in a tight dress and high heels pleading the case center stage. And when the bound-and-gagged, ripped-bodice, helpless, virginal-but-damned-sexy victim character wore thinner than the nightie she was invariably abducted in, she could be replaced with the even more scintillating spandex-clad cat-woman character, whose punches and leg kicks showed off her curves. Over time, the female super-hero or anti-hero has "evolved" to the degree that she is also freely shown *being* hit herself. The violence in both directions has become more real, leaving the heroine looking very much like the old image of victim—bruised, cut, bloody and barely dressed.

On to the commercials, thanks to which basic bodily functions have been introduced as acceptable material for public discourse. Acne and hemorrhoid creme, sanitary products, anxiety medication, and every other remedy or product for any and every real and imagined condition are out there front and center. Women may now be found all across the airwaves frankly discussing formerly unmentionable subjects. I do not deny that on some level this is progress. The time is long past when real, human issues may not be exposed in "polite society." But the time has also passed when we can equate the crashing of taboos with genuine liberation.

What we would like to see now are images of women that are not traditional—by which I mean, that are not the way men traditionally portray women. We want images that are actually realistic—meaning, how women really see themselves and want to be perceived by others. It would be refreshing to see portrayals of women created by women, portrayals of men created by women, and portrayals of men and women created by men who are not invested in the marketing power of pigeonholing and demographics.

I lament the ubiquity of the man's business suit as much as the bright-tight version of professional wear favored by today's on-screen female "role models." In both cases the effect, if not the objective (though I think it *is* the objective), is to strip us of individuality in order to make us more predictable and easily-manipulated consumers. The man's suit and the grooming that goes with it de-sexualize his appearance while imbuing him with the power of conformity to a system in which his "type" is favored. Conversely, the woman's "uniform" and attendant cosmetic enhancements are meant to accentuate her sexuality, so that, however much wealth is evident by her appearance (and it takes considerable resources to look *that* good), she is first and foremost female. The man is a power figure to be followed; the woman is a figure of desire to be pursued.

Each generation that has tried to resist these stock

identities has found itself in yet another battle for self-acceptance, often on the losing side. As more actual women (not the TV kind) reject the fashion dictates of Madison Avenue, the marketing geniuses turn their attention to the men. These days, men are equally the target of commercials intended to make them "need" something special in order to be acceptable. It is now essential that they perfume their bodies, condition their skin, soften (darken or increase) their hair, increase their virility (via medication or the stock market), flatten their tummies, and make themselves more "interesting."

Call me a curmudgeon (she of the tube top, hip-huggers and frizzy hair), but the younger generations' piercing and tattooing backlash to this Madison Avenue version of beauty and grooming looks a lot like self-mutilation. I admit, I'm not getting much traction for my theory that their heavy-metal style represents a deep, internalized self-loathing—certainly not from the young people themselves. One on one, "kids today" strike me as smart, confident and not at all self-hating. Their loathing is directed at societal bullshit and hypocrisy, and it is their right and duty to wage a creative campaign to point out that the emperor has no clothes.

Each generation must fight that battle for primacy in envisioning the world they will inherit. Unfortunately, spontaneous, organic rebellion that emerges within any group these days is quickly trended and friended to death, with the "market" appropriating every new word and gesture for mass franchise. Young people who rejected over-hyped, mass-produced fashion and adorned their very bodies with ink and hardware have seen their style go from fringe to accepted to institutionalized via increasing refinement and reproduction by the purveyors of mass culture. And so we find a relatively new stock character added to the hall of TV types—a goth/punk-styled, geeky young woman. She happens to be very pretty as well as very smart. She is empowered by virtue of her braininess rather than her figure—but let's face it, she still looks like a dress-up doll.

Whether consciously devised or not, mass media entertainment constitutes an effective program of de-sensitization to violence, vulgarity and verbal vicious-ness. The "entertainment" value of violence is mainly in its ability to arrest one's attention. Spend half an hour surfing TV channels (you'll get plenty of movie trailers and video game ads in the mix), and you may come away with PTSD from all the shooting, burning, bombing, slashing, crashing, stalking, dissecting, threatening and torturing you will be offered in the great battle to keep your eyes on the screen.

Likewise, verbal viciousness is sufficiently on display in print, radio and TV "news" that I will not elaborate on the point here, except to note that the nastiness and lies—nothing new, especially in the political arena—are now disseminated with lightning speed, so that resulting disputes may escalate with equal rapidity.

By "vulgarity" I do not refer only to sex debased to something like a joke, or debasing to one or more individuals, but images that are just plain gross and stupid. For example, we now have animated personifications of things like dirt and snot—though that latter word has yet to be used on-air. I suppose actually saying "snot" would be keeping it a bit too real to fulfill the marketing purpose, which is apparently to portray "mucus" (dust, fat cells, germs, stomach acid, ants, roaches, weeds and unsightly growths) as at once cute and killable.

Oh my. Cute and killable. That seems to be the same agenda Madison Avenue has for women. "Here, sweetie, have a cigarette." "Put on this bikini and run for your life." Meanwhile, the straight-laced types you might expect to defend our worth and integrity have fallen back to a notion of female "honor" that relegates us to, 1) the actual role of childbearing and rearing, and 2) its many metaphorical variants in society, such as office mommy—she who props up and cleans up after the overgrown boys in suits.

It would be funny, or it would be irrelevant, except that women are not paid at all for their work in the home, and are not paid equally to men when they work outside of the home. And so we too must exist in a prolonged version of childhood—financially dependent, disempowered, insecure about our identities, uncom-fortable with our bodies, ripe for exploitation. The resulting tension leads to poor relationships between the genders and across generations. This is a battle that no one is winning, though some are banking on it, and laughing all the way. It's been going on at least since someone penned the venerable Adam and Eve tale—and that guy *still* has the pen.

The mass media is a massively wealthy and powerful cadre of elites who literally control the landscape and soundtrack of our lives. How long will we remain "babies," allowing them to drum into us the same simplistic messages of fright or comfort or desire or superiority or insecurity or hostility, like bedtime tales in rotation? Wake up. Grow up. The medium is not the message. We have to take responsibility for the message. Until we do, we'll keep getting the same old fare—reactionary condescension and amoral marketeering designed to make us feel like we're going somewhere, when we're really just tripping over our high heels.

We're All Babies Now
November 20, 2012

Children are cute when they play pretend in grown-up clothes. Set aside any disturbing truths that might be revealed by what the kids choose to imitate of their adult companions' behavior, and enjoy the scene for its adorable innocence. We will find a couple of dynamics at work here on the strictly visual level:

First, we have the well-researched evolutionary attributes of mammals, through which the young possess distinct physical features that adults are hardwired to respond to in a caring, protective manner. These are chiefly a large head out of proportion to the baby body, and large eyes, with small nose and mouth that further accentuate those irresistible "baby blues." We are pre-set to rescue any such appealing little creature in need, whether or not it is related to us. The fact that "all babies look alike" is a survival mechanism of the species. We are inclined to think kids are cute no matter what they are doing or whose they are.

Then there is juxtaposition—the surprising or jarring placement of elements not typically felt to go together. It is a technique used to great effect by Surrealist painters like Salvador Dalí and René Magritte to create dreamlike, disturbing images. A child's figure and face in floppy grown-up clothing is more silly than surreal, and our response is mirth, but the perceptual process is similar. When things that don't generally go together are put together, or when things that do go together are combined in unusual or unexpected ways, that is juxtaposition, and it usually gets our attention.

Kids are cute. Kids dressing up in grown-up clothes are cute. Even when child actors are hired to make an ad in which they are shown playing dress-up, talking about the Mommy and Daddy things that the ad is intended to sell to Mommy and Daddy (or to the child who will lobby Mommy and Daddy), we can still imagine young children playing this game of their own volition and smile at their cuteness. Using cute kids (or pets) seems a harmless gimmick to keep our eyes on the screen.

The baby stock-trader character is a different matter. There is nothing either natural or believable about the baby talking cogently about anything, let alone stocks. We know the baby is real (cute) but the voice is dubbed, and the image is manipulated digitally to sync the words of a male actor to the baby's mouth movements. The juxtaposition here requires a combination of visual and aural elements. We look at the baby, which stimulates our instinct to nurture and protect, while at the same time we hear the adult male voice. Creepy.

Let's look at the subtext of this ad series:

1) It suggests that the electronic trading service is so simple that a baby can use it, which by extension implies that the consumer is not much smarter than a baby.

2) It makes the product seem innocent and harmless.

3) It suggests that anyone who might try to prevent you from using the product is a Mean Mommy and should be ignored. In short: Baby knows best. And if Madison Avenue can get you to surrender your critical judgment to an animated baby, then you are ripe to buy into just about anything they can pitch your way. Score!

Now, what has been the natural evolution of the baby who speaks with an adult voice? Duh—grown-ups who talk like children. A recent ad campaign that comes to mind features office workers teasing and cajoling each other like children, in childish voices, in order to get to eat the latest greatest fast food concoction. One should infer it is not really food an adult would want. Possibly the ad is targeted at preteens and teenagers to play off their anxieties and aspirations going into adulthood, while at the same time reinforcing childish cravings and lack of inhibitions. Let's face it, a mature ability to delay gratification is not what advertisers want of us. This ad campaign, and one that preceded it in which young parents are so agog at a new soft drink that they fill the kitchen with cases of soda while ignoring their children, represent a blatant effort to de-condition grown-up reasoning, and to inhibit its cultivation in those currently approaching adulthood.

Look at the whole of the advertising landscape on TV, not just product by product, and you will see a growing trend toward turning babies into grownups and grownups into babies, toward generally softening up our impulse control and critical decision-making ability. What could be better for the sellers of things we don't need or can't afford, or that may be downright bad for us, than to enable all of our most childish qualities while empowering actual children to have a say—by depicting them as having a say—in purchasing decisions?

Look, we all know that if something is an easy sell because it's needed, it works, and everyone knows about it—like a broom—you don't have to put a lot of effort into advertising it. Advertising is intended to befuddle, startle, stimulate, agitate—anything to get your attention and create a need or desire where there was none before. But there are deeply troubling aspects to the blurring of babyhood and adulthood in our mass-media culture, not the least of which is this: Children need the protection and care of adults; much of what is shown on TV is not appropriate for certain age groups; it is therefore not healthy or helpful to short-circuit the rationality and authority of those adults responsible for supervising the screen time of children.

Breaking Down by Degrees, Holiday Mood Swings, & the Zombie Shopper Apocalypse
November 28, 2012

This year's pre-Thanksgiving media buzz focused on the move by some retailers to open on Thanksgiving. This was framed as a violation of the Black Friday "tradition" and the unique National Secular Holiday status that Thanksgiving holds. Serious labor problems were spotlighted as Walmart workers protested being made to work on the holiday. In her article "The grinches who stole Black Friday" Esther J. Cepeda wrote eloquently about the disgusting madness of Black Friday itself and the sick eagerness of compliant, complicit consumers to embrace every extension of their shopping opportunities, no matter the consequences for workers, families and all that is right and good in America...

But, hold on there—two days later, the experiment was deemed a success. Look at those sales figures! Look at those tallies of bodies in the stores! It was the blackest Black Friday (and Thursday) ever. Now, you tell me what's good for America!

And then, as though struck by a horrible sugar crash after too much pumpkin pie and ice cream, the National Spirit was down in the dumps again because...

The War on Christmas is back! Those secularist socialist atheists want to take away all of the fun, the lights, the Magi, the Marys and Josephs and Baby Jesuses. They want to replace special *words*, to replace *Christmas* with the bland, inclusive *Holiday*. Where is the respect for tradition, for the rituals of the season that we have held so dear, for so long? (Like Black Friday?) Where will it all end?

I'll tell you where I *hope* it ends—imagine: Stores will be open or closed on Thanksgiving as suits their business, the same way they set store hours all the rest of the year, and they will organize their staffing and staff benefits accordingly. There will be a gradual dilution of the Black Friday storm-the-stores syndrome. Business will be evened out across the year, making holiday sales less critical while increasing revenues, jobs and demand for product overall through innovative use of on-line and brick-and-mortar sales strategies. The true spirit of Christmas will return to the hearts and hearths of those who celebrate the birth of Jesus, and the fake crap will recede. A genuine, general, winter season-of-giving spirit will spread respect and concern for all humanity. Amen.

This was originally headed in a very different direction! I planned to say that "by degrees" the forces of consumerism were taking down our defenses against the marketing madness. Store openings on Black Friday inching earlier and earlier, leading to Thanksgiving Day hours, the Internet allowing 24/7 shopping—I was on board with those decrying the relentless assault on consumers and the all-too-effective campaign to turn America into a nation of Pavlovian shoppers, marching mindlessly and soullessly to the stores at the ring of a bell. ("We have seen the Zombie Apocalypse and it is us.")

But then it dawned on me—this is a good thing. No, not the Zombie Shopper Apocalypse, but the demystification of Black Friday, the weakening of the grip of "holidays" on our public lives, the eventual severing of the link between the supposedly secular Thanksgiving and the supposedly religious celebration of Christmas. By degrees, the stores are diminishing the Black Friday phenomenon, and I think wisely so. They can stay open 24/7 all the way from Halloween to New Year's as far as I'm concerned (then I can shop for shoes in peace some 2 a.m.). Think of all the *jobs*.

As for the War-on-Christmas folks, they should get used to losing. By degrees, everything that has come to represent that traditional White Christmas fantasy is breaking down, in large part due to the capitalist excess they and their "conservative" brethren champion right alongside their "U.S. founded as a Christian Nation" assertions. The toys are made in China, more moms and dads are without work, our extravagant energy consumption creates pollution that sullies the wintry scene; arts and crafts are replaced by mass media (often not child-friendly) and mass production, and consumed in pixels and bits instead of in person.

By degrees, the old ways fall aside and new ways take their place. What do you want to spend your energy on—fighting a fake war on fake things, or finding out for yourself what is meaningful to you out of all the clutter and noise, and preserving it in your heart and your home? Nothing is taking away our freedom or right to treasure and care for our own traditions in private and in public in the U.S. You put your tree in the window, Mom will put her menorah in the window. Even we naturalists will put a candle in the window to mark the winter solstice. By degrees, light and sanity will return. One day we will step forth from our shelters and the Zombie Shopper Apocalypse will be over.

Gun Sex
December 4, 2012

Not too long ago I heard a passing reference to *The Man Who Fell To Earth*, filmed right here in New Mexico, and decided I had better see it. This 1976 movie is sufficiently flawed to make me hesitate to recommend it, but at the same time it contains such a sharp, prescient, uncompromising critique of American culture that I feel obliged to encourage everyone to have a look. There are a number of aspects worthy of discussion, but one scene in particular demands to be addressed here, as it contains an explicit depiction of exactly the joining of violence and sex that I and many other feminists have been writing about.

The climactic scene comes near the end of the film (though the end at that point was not as near as I had hoped). Our doomed alien hero has not succeeded in returning to his drought-devastated planet. He has been trapped by government agents, and is alternately tortured and pampered, numbed by booze and media. When the woman who loved him (for being so different, until she found out how really different he was) is sent back to him, their sex play starts anew. Suddenly he pulls a gun on her— Taunts her, and— Pulls the trigger, and— BANG! Big noise, but no blood! Hysterical relief from both of them. He explains that he had asked his keepers for a gun with blanks, and they obliged. He shoots at her. BANG! BANG! She shoots at him. They giggle and squeal, wrestle and lick and kick. Two slim, pale, naked bodies, and a shiny, heavy pistol. BANG! BANG! They are literally having a blast.

Of course, with today's sensibilities—that is, if I were watching a movie made recently—one or more of those bangs would probably not be a blank, and the scene would end with white sheets and pale bodies drenched in blood and gore. This is what one has come to expect. But here, they are all blanks. The fun is genuine if desperate, and apparently heralds the release of the stranded alien, as if he has proven with his debauchery his full assimilation into the human species. All the way fallen, reduced to a state of lethargic impotence, he is no longer a threat; all stirrings of desire can be pacified with violent fantasy sex play, actual or vicarious.

That scene is one helluva statement. It is not sexy. It is scary and sad. If the movie were made today, the woman's body would be much fuller and bouncier—a veritable sex bomb that would heighten the prurience while lessening the realism and intensity of the scene;

and the male body would either be really ripped, or hardly shown at all. More likely, the entire scene would be cut for fear of adult ratings and reduced revenues.

Everything today is so much more polished and self-conscious than the gritty works of the 70s. Hollywood is very careful to isolate elements even as they are being combined. Guns here, girls there; shooting here, screwing there. It's like the latest in *haute cuisine* in which everything is deconstructed into separate tasty bites. Violence and sex may come in alternating waves, often presented in alluring proximity to each other (our half-clad hostage cowering before a male with a weapon, or the half-clad warrior woman actually wielding the weapon) but the stimulation is all of a piece—arousal— and we know they are meant to go together. It's the mass media's great orgiastic fantasy feast of Gun Sex. *The Man Who Fell To Earth* gave it to us bluntly, literally and surely sarcastically—but I could not look at it and laugh.

Guns and sex do not go together. Sex is a healthy, natural act that one can hope to take part in with affection, pleasure and some regularity. Guns have no place whatsoever in my life and the daily lives of most civilians, yet we see guns and gun violence on TV routinely verging on monotonously. Maybe if the networks could show more sex, they'd show less violence. They're just looking for ways to get and keep our eyes on their product. But think about it: Sex is more appealing in person than on the screen, while gun violence is not at all entertaining if you are actually in the middle of it. Putting the two together—unlike mixing your peas and potatoes—does not make a happy or healthy or desirable combination.

The Man Who Fell To Earth suggests that we needn't worry too much about defending Earth from extra-terrestrial invasion. If we lack adequate technology to fight the aliens, we'll still be able to kill their souls with our culture.

[I originally published this essay under the following note: *This post was in the pipeline before the murder over the weekend of Kasandra Perkins by Jovan Belcher, which was newsworthy mainly for its impact on professional football. Such an occurrence is otherwise so unremarkable as to be relegated to the commonplace by the label "domestic violence." It's a private matter, really, unless it interrupts our Sunday sport. From* Gun Violence Statistics *at the Futures Without Violence web site: "Nearly one-third of all women murdered in the United States in recent years were murdered by a current or former intimate partner. In 2000, 1,247 women, more than three a day, were killed by their intimate partners."* (futureswithoutviolence.org)]

Women Must Take the Lead in Ending Gun Violence
December 16, 2012

Women Must Take the Lead in Ending Gun Violence. *Why?* Because our "protection" is so often cited as justification for one or more family members to arm themselves and bring weapons into the home. Because every shooter has a mother. Because most shooters end up dead, and too often their mothers or the mothers of their children do too.

Because "building a strong economy that supports working families" is trotted out whenever an industry senses that new regulations are coming, but gun violence destroys families immediately and irrevocably. Implementing tougher rules for buying and selling firearms is not going to leave bodies littered in the aisles either at the moment or in the future, though not doing so will. We had a Federal Assault Weapons Ban for ten years (1994-2004) and it did not bring down the economy. Why was it allowed to expire?

Women Must Take the Lead in Ending Gun Violence. *How?* How did the NRA gain so much clout? With money, by funding the campaigns of lawmakers who would do their bidding or at least be "sympathetic" to their interests (read "spineless").

Women have economic clout as well. The web site she-conomy.com contains a wealth of information about the wealth of U.S. women and their buying power. According to their Quick Facts page, more than 80 percent of all consumer purchasing decisions are made by women. Now that we are in the season of heightened shopping and buying, women can immediately start showing their displeasure with gun culture by avoiding general retailers that sell military-grade weapons and ammunition alongside the groceries, clothing and toys.

We can also reject TV shows, movies and games (and their paraphernalia) that glorify violence. Anyone would be devastated if there was a shoot-out in their home—so why do we willingly allow such scenes to blast out of our recreational media? (If you have trouble finding anything on TV that isn't full of shooting, screaming, smashing and explosions or—even more troubling in some ways—merely peppered with graphic ads for same, may I suggest Animal Planet's *Too Cute Kittens* and *Too Cute Puppies*.)

Are you mailing out season's greetings actually or electronically? Add your state and national congressional delegations to the list, and let them know that you are wishing for tougher gun control and fewer gun maimings and deaths in the coming year.

Women Must Take the Lead in Ending Gun Violence. *But it's not our fault!* Exactly. We cannot expect the grown-up boys with their deadly toys to end this game of their own volition. The disproportionate number of men in top level executive and creative positions in the entertainment industry correlates to the disproportionate amount of gun violence in our media. This in turn has a correlation to the acceptance, even glamor, of guns in our culture. Women must seek equal representation in all positions of influence over government and society so that our perspectives are given equal weight and consideration. Of course I welcome men of peace and reason to this cause, but my message here is that U.S. women have not been heard on the issue of gun violence.

I'm not suggesting that women are powerless. We have been admitted to most of the halls of power and influence—in small numbers and provided we play by the rules previously established by the male elite. We have a foot in the door, but we're still spending way too much energy trying to push through, when we have so much more to offer.

I'm not saying that women are better by nature than men. We are different biologically and we are different by virtue of the gender roles permitted or imposed on us by society. I can't imagine how anyone who has a sympathetic heart and a moral conscience can look at a world in which innocents are killed by a crazed gunman—or by a suicide bomber, or a drone attack, or preventable disease or starvation or exposure—and not wish it were different. So maybe it's time to approach things differently. Women can provide different perspectives.

A gun does not have rights. All guns are not equal.

Guns are destructive by design, and they have their uses. They should come under at least as much regulation as vehicles, alcohol and narcotics. Remember that it was women who stepped forward to lead the campaign against drunk driving. Mothers Against Drunk Driving was formed in 1980; according to their statistics, alcohol-related driving fatalities had dropped from 30,000 annually to under 17,000 by 2005. Take a look at the M.A.D.D. web site (madd.org) and see how they did it. Notice that they haven't put an end to either the alcoholic beverage industry or the auto industry. They made our streets safer.

We need to have sane gun control policy to make our streets, homes, schools and public spaces safer. We won't get it until we change the culture. To do that we will have to face down propaganda and fear mongering from those who are deadly serious, as well as the "all in fun" or "just in it for the bucks" desensitization and glamorization by entertainment moguls.

Macho gun culture has had its day (century, millennium). It's time for women to stop feeling embarrassed or befuddled or bullied into going along with it. Men who kill with guns also die by them. Women must stop enabling, take responsibility for our own power, and step up to the task of undoing the supremacy of the gun.

Bill Baird, My Hero and My Friend
December 22, 2012

There are genuine heroes in the world, and Bill Baird is one of them. You can pretty much tell who the good guys are by how much they are vilified. Those who actually succeed in their righteous cause generally enjoy such rewards as death threats, historical rewrites, media blackouts and loss of income. Bill has endured all of that and more.

I was fifteen in 1972 when Bill Baird won the first of three landmark Supreme Court cases granting rights and freedoms relating to birth control and sexuality to single people, teenagers and gay people. I was not unaware of the firestorm surrounding the issue of abortion (Baird's NY clinic was literally firebombed) and the controversial Bill Baird. By the time I entered college—in Boston, where in 1967 Baird got himself arrested in order to argue for single people's rights to birth control—my access to birth control was unquestioned. I don't think I even imagined that an unmarried woman would not have had that legal right just a few years prior.

Those were heady days for young people with short memories. We were riding the tail of a cultural revolution that had dashed racial barriers, bashed gender roles, and felt close to crashing the glass ceiling. We got the benefits of those fights without getting beat up or worn down. We hadn't any sense of the reactionary drag that would come to bear on the vessel we expected to sail into the new age.

Fast forward to 2011. I was attending the national conference of the American Humanist Association, and looking over the schedule at breakfast. I had circled Bill Baird's talk, because the name clicked when I read his bio. Here was the legendary man himself.

"Oh, Bill Baird...he's gotten kind of bitter. I think I will go to..." one of my breakfast companions said, naming another speaker. I put a big asterisk next to the session I had already circled. It proved to be one of the most enlightening, inspiring ninety minutes of my life.

Was Bill bitter? Well, he certainly had harsh words for the humanists, the feminists, for Planned Parenthood, the ACLU and our own AHA among others, all the groups that had spurned him while he was fighting an unpopular fight with unpopular tactics. (Here he held up an enlarged black and white photo of a woman who has died on a tiled kitchen floor from a botched home abortion.)

The stories poured out of him—beatings, arrests, threats, repudiation; loss of family, friendships and professional career; and the personal fortune earned from that career expended on legal battles fought not for himself—a successful, professional, fully empowered, white male—but for us. For women. For humanity. Clearly what hurt the most was the questioning of his motives. Why would a man put his life on the line for women, blacks and the poor? He was suspect on all fronts—an infiltrator trying to subvert the women's movement; a commie; an atheist; a racist who wanted to bring birth control to the inner city in order to reduce the black population; a womanizer on the make! When in truth he was only ever a humanist, a humanitarian intent on saving lives, a patriot dedicated to defending the highest ideals of our country.

Bill is still a warrior. He's rough, he's rude, he's righteous. He's full of fight. But today, at 80, he's fighting for the record, for respect, for acknowledgment of the role he played—at great personal cost—in laying the groundwork for *Roe v. Wade*. He is nearing the end of his hardworking days, a wounded hero whose legacy just happens to be crucially relevant to today's conversation about women's health and reproductive rights.

Which brings us to the present. I recently contacted Bill and his wife Joni, in my capacity as co-chair of the AHA Feminist Caucus, to ask if Bill would help us raise awareness about the ERA by issuing a statement with some historical perspective. Joni relayed the emails back and forth and offered insightful comments of her own. What are we trying to do? What are we trying to say? We got to know each other a little.

And then Bill Baird called me. My hero. Our hero. He prefaced the statement on the ERA below with a careful explication of true humanism, in which we all work for the liberation of each other, not just "our own oppressed group"—"We need to remove self-imposed barriers. It's people helping people. I don't have to be black to support black people"—and a rapid-fire complaint about feminists who can't acknowledge the men who have been on their side, and the sacrifices men have made for women's rights.

Following up in a later conversation, Bill would say to me, "You tell me who's bitter. Why would they try to write me out of history? I am not bitter, I am wounded." He was not speaking metaphorically. Nothing about this story is metaphorical. The blood and gore of desperate women, the pain and fear of his own incarceration and abuse were all too real, and traumatize to this day.

Heroes, by definition, are powerful characters. They can be as unnerving to those they defend as they are to those they battle. We may feel uneasy being indebted to them. I can see how a previous generation of feminists may not have wanted a wealthy white male—the epitome of the patriarchal establishment—jumping into the fray to act as their champion. But let's be honest. Who else was going to do it? Who, at the time, had the resources, the confidence—and, yes, the balls—to do what Bill Baird did? He was our champion. We needed him. We still need him, because unfortunately the advancements he fought for are slipping away. Fortunately, he is still here for us.

Heroes do exist. It would serve us well to look past the battle scars, learn their stories, and thank them for all they've won for us—by defending those gains with equal courage, conviction and passion.

Statement on the ERA from Bill Baird

My U.S. Supreme Court case *Baird v. Eisenstadt* legalized birth control nationally on March 22, 1972. *Baird* was quoted 6 times in *Roe v. Wade* and in my two other U.S. Supreme Court cases, *Baird v. Bellotti I* and *Baird v. Bellotti II* for minor's rights to abortion.

For nearly 50 years I fought against anti-birth control and anti-abortion laws that have enslaved women for centuries often resulting in poverty, illness and even death. The suffering that I witnessed when abortion and birth control were illegal propels me to continue to fight for the equality of women and all of humankind.

I fervently believe that the Equal Rights Amendment must be passed so that women can be on an equal playing field with men in our nation. It is a national disgrace that this battle for equality continues into the 21st century. Women must be granted permanent equal rights in our U.S. Constitution.

This mission is more pressing than ever given the lack of clarity and consistency from those holding and running for political office. With only three more states left to ratify this vital constitutional affirmation for women's rights, let all of us working together usher in a new era of equality for all Americans.

[To learn more about Bill and Joni Baird's important work, visit prochoiceleague.org.]

Where Are the Voices for the ERA?
January 22, 2013

A lot of breath has been expended today on the 40th anniversary of *Roe v. Wade*. I wonder why no one bothered to mention that we are 90 years since the introduction of the Equal Rights Amendment, and how passage of the ERA would provide constitutional guarantee to women that our rights cannot be abridged on the basis of sex.

Roe v. Wade, and the Bill Baird cases before and after, established that sexual conduct and reproductive choice are protected by virtue of our right to privacy— such personal matters are not the government's business. The Constitution also grants us the right to worship, speak, publish, and assemble without interference from the government, and further specifies that the government cannot establish a state religion. Given that objections to contraception spring from religious positions that we do not all share, and which the government is not permitted to impose on us, we should not even be having an argument about abortion, let alone tolerating state restrictions on any aspect of health care for women.

Why don't women enjoy the same right to privacy and autonomy of our persons as men? Imagine the states trying to legislate what men may and may not do about their reproductive health? Guys can't even abide having their phallic *symbols* restricted. (You know, guns.)

103

When will women—and men—of every sexual orientation and gender identity be able to turn to a Constitutional Amendment for recourse against misogynists and moralizers, just as people of color are able to challenge racial discrimination under the 15th Amendment?

Repeat after me: ERA

The ERA simply forbids discrimination on the basis of sex, meaning that it expands everyone's rights and protections under the Constitution. A number of groups are working very hard to finally make the ERA the law of the land. Why aren't we hearing about it?

I am genuinely shocked and disappointed that in the entire raft of liberal talkers, not a one has had the gumption, or maybe even the notion, that we can do more than wring our hands over denial of access to abortion and contraception. In the big picture, those attacks on women's rights are unconstitutional. *That* should be the context of the discussion; and the ERA should be the remedy put forward and discussed.

[ERA update: The ERA was ratified by Nevada on March 22, 2017 and by Illinois on May 30, 2018. Ratification by one more state, to make a total of 38, will meet the requirement that Amendments to the Constitution be approved by three-quarters of the states.]

Wake Up to Your Media Landscape
February 13, 2013

Humanity in the 21st century—what is our new frontier? You could say it's technology, but in many ways we've mastered that already. We can create pretty much anything we can conceive of in the way of gadgets large and small, simple and complex. If we haven't done it yet, we're working on it; and if we haven't thought of it yet, it's only a matter of time before we do.

Our challenge is to exist as healthy, harmonious, self-determined humans within the new virtual world shaped by our technology. Who is in charge here? What determines the sensory inputs of my day? Who determines those?

My postage-stamp backyard yet breathes with the quiet and quickening rhythms of nature, a surprising variety when I can be still enough to observe. But my attention is mostly riveted to a screen, which is often streaming with messages and images sequenced and juxtaposed with relentless randomness or actual intent to befuddle. Either way, I'll be multi-tasking my way to not doing anything vital at all if I'm not careful.

Click, play, watch, listen, comment, like, friend, invite, meet-up, tweet, retweet, blog, reblog, send, check, send, check, send, like, like, like. Thoughts are involved, relationships, ideas and information. But the intriguing stuff is getting sliced and diced into thinner and more mixed-up segments all the time. The mixing up of inputs is as troublesome as their speed and brevity.

In previous centuries, artist-scientists turned their attention to the natural world. True, they and all of humanity had always existed within it, but the organizing thoughts of civilization had previously focused on spiritual ideas about supernatural forces that directed human activity. Our inquisitive types decided to look to the evidence of the natural world for insight into the way things actually worked. They began to carefully document their observations in pictures and words. These could be compared and studied with a degree of objectivity; theories derived; suppositions tested; and future effects predicted.

Artistic expression and scientific exploration have always been with us, inherent inclinations of the human mind that cannot be suppressed. Once we woke up to the patterns and processes of the natural world in which we exist, there would be no going back. We came to a broad consensus about "the real world" and, with or without lingering spiritual feelings, we have been living in it ever since.

Until lately. Now we are in a virtual world. Not the stuff of spirits but of bits—magic of another sort. It has its own lore and legend, priests and rituals, cults and sects (and lots and lots of sex). The deciders of culture would like to establish their current power as unassailable by shaping the way the memes are streamed, and then making that seem inevitable. ("Every drama on TV includes gun violence because that's what the viewers want, look at these ratings.") They widened a country lane to a highway and now feel entitled to send any and every piece of junk down it they please, followed by a parade telling us how much we liked it.

Fortunately, a new generation of inquisitive, independent thinkers is taking an objective look at the mass media landscape with all of its component parts, and documenting their findings for all. And just like their artist-naturalist predecessors, they are demonstrating a process of examination and critique that we can all engage in and benefit from—in the same way our counterparts in past times (up to the present), while not biologists themselves, kept their garden notes and birdwatching journals.

We call today's discipline Media Literacy, and once you get the hang of paying attention to the design and details of mass media messages, it will always be with you. At that point, you will find yourself having more of an opinion about, and exercising more control over, your personal media "backyard" and, I hope, contributing to an improved media ecosystem for all of us.

What I love about the study of mass media is that while there is a great deal of academic work going on, the principles are quite easy for anyone at any age to understand, apply and share. Whatever your background, you will find a welcoming and vibrant community at any Media Education event.

Still Stewing About *Makers*
March 15, 2013

I've been remiss in not commenting on significant items that have been in the news lately. Insults and attacks on the fundamental rights of women are escalating alongside our protests of same. And such action that comes amid much back-patting by one group or another generally amounts to nothing more than shining a spotlight on hideous behaviors and their tragic results, with the promise that "this time we will act." Lip service is on the rise for such causes as ending violence against women in civilian and military realms, regulating guns and gun ownership, improving access to healthcare and education, reducing the disparity between rich and poor (of which women and children are disproportionately among the poor), and limiting the power corporations have over our political process. But it mostly amounts to the staking out of entrenched positions at the expense of finding real solutions. One simply becomes loath to add to the sound and fury.

The recent multi-hour PBS documentary on the history of the women's movement should have been balm to our beleaguered feminist spirits, but it had a strange effect on me, and the more I think about it, the grumpier I get. Even the title *Makers* puts me on edge. I suppose someone thought it was clever to tie up the traditional role of homemaker, women's entry into the industrial age as factory workers, and the emergence of revolutionary history-makers in this neat little bow, but it cuts to the element of gender-race-class subjugation that has always offended me most: the assumption that some people are naturally bred to be scholars, thinkers and leaders, while others of us are consigned to be makers and caregivers—in short, mindless worker bees.

As for the style and substance of the *Makers* documentary, I did find the material engrossing, often moving, and I welcomed every scrap of information offered. Yet I also felt there was something pat and superficial about it, especially when it came to modern times that I have lived through, and detailed (or left out) some characters whom I have actually recently met or learned about in the context of my own feminist leadership role.

By the end of the series, I sensed that I had been witness to history in the process of being sanitized. There was the inevitable Hollywood glow around everything, and an undue perkiness in which the worst affronts to women could be placed squarely, if unrealistically, in the past tense. I couldn't help feeling like the ostensible objectivity, and therefore "for the record" cachet that goes with anything on public television and radio, had been appropriated to convey what will now amount to an "official" version of what the feminist movement was and will be.

Who got to write that history? It's time to stop kidding ourselves about the autonomy and impartiality of public broadcasting. They have corporate sponsors versus advertisers, but "corporate" is the operative word. Content is adjusted to make wealthy sponsors happy, though it may work slightly differently than on for-profit networks. Maybe you have noticed these trends when you watch PBS or listen to NPR:

* Segments are shorter.

* Excessive time is spent repeatedly hyping each upcoming segment, which diminishes the substantive content of the segment itself.

* Simple statements of who sponsored the segments have expanded into actual ad-speak.

* Anything that might be controversial or inflammatory is abbreviated, diluted, scored with obtrusive soundtrack, and recited breezily by narrators who have a perpetual smile—if not snark—in their voices.

* These "difficult" pieces are then surrounded by mindless pop culture and audience participation fluff, so you can forget them as quickly as possible.

* The reporters-commentators eschew neutrality in their tone and questions in favor of gushing emotionality; they often answer their own question and consume most of the available interview time on their own thoughts and phrasing, versus letting the interviewee speak; they generally seem to prefer cutting and pasting together a pre-planned composition instead of actively probing for new information and deeper understanding of the subject at hand.

I'm in a funk because, between *Makers* and all the *mishegas* that has transpired since, I feel overwhelmed by the variety and scope of insults to my intelligence and sensibilities perpetrated by media, politicians, and well-meaning activists alike. So, let's talk honestly about feminism, the women's movement, and the broader movement to win equality and justice for everyone.

In the first place, it just hurts to confront and truly digest the fact that you have come into the world as a hated class. I don't say that lightly. It's absurd on its face, but it's true. Ask the required-to-be-celibate pope. Ask the male-only-need-apply cardinals who chose him, cloistered away in their scarlet gowns and attended to by faceless nuns.

Ask the military mucky-mucks who think they can write off rape and assault within their own ranks as just part of the job, or the armies of the world who use rape as a weapon of war.

Ask the evangelical preachers and holier-than-thou politicians who can't abide the idea of women earning equal wages for work outside the home, because it would cut into all of the free labor they are expected to provide for the household.

Ask Hollywood, where the torture and terrorization of women in their plot-lines amounts to a conditioning regimen in which women learn to expect and accept that sexual violence or threat of it must be a factor in any crime against them, while men are encouraged to mentally practice and fantasize about all the ways in which women can be demeaned, used, and *put in their place*.

Ask the supposedly pious, life-loving people who think a collection of womb-dependent cells has more value and "right to life" than the mature human being who may or may not be prepared for a pregnancy.

To really and truly absorb the historic subjugation of women, the tenacity of misogynist attitudes up to today, and the tenuous position women still endure—that we have so little representation in government, business, religious and social institutions that we are literally ruled by men in every area of our lives—chills me to my core.

I have been fortunate in that I never felt that my family, friends and professional associates hated me or demeaned me for being a woman. This only makes it more of a shock to the system to realize what, in fact, over the course of generations, society had intended my lot in life to be as a female: restricted; controlled; financially dependent; psychologically and often physically, violently muscled into subservience, sexual servitude and the virtual slavery of providing free domestic labor. In short, there was to be no regard for personal preference or individual potential.

People in power are still trying to impose this role on women, and in many cases they are succeeding. We continue to be impoverished, exploited and subject to chauvinistic whim and damaging mind games from both male and female adherents to gender role tradition.

It makes me sick. The fact that I feel like I've been here before contributes to my dizzy, nauseated feeling of betrayal and disillusionment. . . .

A kid on the playground told the little Jewish girl that she would go to hell for not believing in Jesus. It was so startling and ridiculous to the pampered six-year-old that she could laugh it off. . . . But it sank in over time, as she learned how that attitude played out in history, as the reality of genocide was hammered home. People can hate you, and kill you, for some trait that doesn't even define you as the individual you are, for something you had no control over. As if knowing the history wasn't bad enough, the girl came to realize that the haters were still out there, some of them still had power to harm her kind. But, this thing that she was, that she didn't choose, that they hated her for—being a Jew—guess what? Her "kind" were no kinder! They branded her too. They decreed a lesser role and opportunities for her too. They'd call her a sinner too—unclean. Because she was female. And this was the culture and identity she was supposed to cling to against those other oppressors?

I keep coming back to the word "betrayed." This is where women stand today, just like yesterday and the day before. It's what happens when your destiny is not in your own hands—those who have power over you either take care of you or betray you.

Men still dictate what the lives of women are. We lucky ones, who have been able to assert our independence, who have been able to laugh off the odd sexist remark or unwelcome advance here and there, must look beyond our immediate circumstances to acknowledge what is still reality for most women, and call it for what it is: complete and utter betrayal of the fundamental personhood of women, with little indication that society as a whole is ready or willing to cast off its patriarchal hierarchy. That hurts, and no amount of pep in the soundtrack, or congratulatory recapitulations of "progress" in the script of *Makers* could soften that blow for me.

I recently wrote in an email to fellow feminists, "A world full of war and poverty is not one in which women have had an equal say." Women do not engage in this battle for equality for ourselves alone. The only way humanity is going to "make it" is together, hand in hand, in mutual respect, with concerted effort, and with every bit of talent and ingenuity that each of us can muster.

If I Could Convince You of Only One Thing, It Would Be This: Value Yourself
April 21, 2013

I am often overwhelmed by all of the alerts and calls to action that come through my email, and I wonder about my own message. Is everyone as inured to my lectures about feminism and media literacy as I am to their barrage of equally worthy appeals? And what are the chances that someone who doesn't agree with my position will be won over, if they even bother to read what I have to say? We each have our own soapbox these days, but we are mostly preaching to the choir, now that the public space is virtual and everybody can customize their path through it to find only "likes" and avoid anything they don't like.

Even among my friends in the feminist-humanist movement, there are vast differences of opinion on key issues. And it is so unfulfilling—after the flush of ego exhilaration wears off—to keep debating and preaching and cajoling in this realm of competitive opining. I want to share something with you that is unequivocal, nonpartisan, positive and universal. Thus I have decided that if I could convince you, all of you, each of you, of just one thing, it would be to value yourself.

I am not talking about acquiring confidence or even self-esteem, and certainly not a sense of superiority or entitlement. Valuing oneself has to do with appreciating one's own uniqueness and feeling committed to exploring that potential. Smugness is really antithetical to valuing oneself, because it implies you've "arrived" and can coast the rest of the way. Smugness is not a survival skill. A degree of humility and flexibility is needed to adapt as times change.

Care enough about yourself to be open to criticism, advice and differing perspectives. You owe it to yourself to keep that ego in its place and your wits limber. At the same time, don't put yourself in a mindset in which you can be crushed by what other people think, say or do. There are any number of external measures by which the world will judge you, and crush you. When you value yourself, you don't have to get caught up in all of that.

I implore you—do not ever let yourself be crushed by the judgment of others or your own thoughts. Have a good cry and then get up and battle on. (Maybe take a nap in between—always works for me.) You have something no one else has, and you may not even know what it is yet, or what to do with it, but when you decide it's worth your while to look into that, you'll feel rewarded with or without the approval of others.

Value being alone with yourself to think your own thoughts.

Value your privacy.

Value your dignity.

Value your gut instincts.

Value your individuality. You are not a statistic or a label, you are you.

Value your physical self and your inherent beauty.

Value your intellect and common sense.

Value your values. Never let someone else convince you to set aside your good judgment or ethical standards.

Value your capacity to grow and change. Trust your ability to manage, and even to find something better if your work or personal relationship jeopardizes your safety or has become offensive to you.

Value yourself enough to say No, when serving others detracts from your own important pursuits.

Value yourself enough to say Yes, when people who see your value ask for your help.

That's it. That's all I want to convince you to do, think, feel. Because I'm convinced that when we value ourselves, think for ourselves, stand up for ourselves, stop allowing ourselves to be bullied, demeaned and manipulated, the R*E*S*P*E*C*T quotient goes up in the world, and that's good for everyone.

Part 3

A Kind of Hope

Selected Essays from the
Humanist Society of New Mexico *Newsletter*
January 2013 – October 2014

Let's Keep Going
January 2013

If you are reading this newsletter, then we have survived another doomsday prophecy and must carry on with humanity. I'm sure that will not be a disappointment to humanists, though I did detect an air of hopefulness among end-of-the-world predictors. From religious doctrines about End Times, Armageddon, the destruction that must presage messianic renewal, to the secular offerings of Hollywood, we can observe a longing—if not to end it all already, then at least to practice the end.

Let's look at all those movies that are made about grand disasters. Aside from the entertainment value (if you're into that sort of thing) of meteor crashes, alien invasion, nuclear apocalypse, tidal waves, earthquakes, etc., these fictions give us a chance to rehearse our practical, ethical and emotional responses to dire circumstances. The screenplays typically suggest that the survival of humankind depends on the survival of a few exceptional individuals or small groups, while all the rest of the teeming masses may be swept away. Their lost lives are available for inspiration, motivation and dedication to renewal, while their high-maintenance physical presence has been conveniently eliminated along with the cancerous urban-industrial landscape.

Real life is a little more complicated than that and not readily reconfigured with the stroke of the scriptwriter's pen. The problems we face as a society ultimately boil down to the workings of human psychology, which is still driven in large part by fear, physical cravings, and possessiveness regardless of how much security we achieve. Humanists may be inclined to wonder if our species can evolve fast enough, intellectually and emotionally, to achieve a genuinely fair and mutually respectful society before we blow ourselves up or poison the planet to the point that it will no longer sustain human life. Adherents to inflexible doctrines, whether religious, political or economic, may be more likely to indulge in a fatalistic wish to actually or metaphorically wipe it all away and start anew. As I write, Congress is contemplating "going over the cliff" and "taking the nuclear option."

Is *kaboom!* really our only choice? Sure, things get messy when you've got a lot of sentient life kicking around. Our methods for dealing with personal desires and decisions are murky; group consensus, if we can achieve it at all, is tenuous. So many things are beyond our control—all of history, for a start. So, do we exert such control as we have over the future through violent, destructive, irreversible acts? I suppose there is a comforting certainty to being wiped out, hitting rock bottom. One's priorities at that point have been greatly simplified and clarified.

Perhaps the urge to keep starting over, to back up or undo modern developments, is simply a failure of vision.

We know what collapse looks like. We know what survival looks like. We also know what flourishing societies look like, and how they become corrupted. Do we yet know what sustainable success for our species looks like?

Humanists are involved in imaging and pursuing that agreeable, sustainable future. We are not hurtling toward the end times but finding our way toward better times—with curiosity, creativity, caring, reason and hope.

Plus we have fun. Thanks for a great 2012, everyone. Let's keep going!

Drawin' for Darwin
February 2013

The February 12 anniversary of Charles Darwin's birth provides opportunity to consider the importance of Art to human civilization. Yes, we will celebrate Darwin's rigorous investigative method and how his theory of evolution by natural selection has contributed to our knowledge in every branch of Science. But, I ask you: How widely would Darwin's research and theory be understood without the Art—without the many detailed drawings of the fossils he collected, and the illustrations commissioned by him and his collaborating authors for *The Zoology of the Voyage of H.M.S. Beagle*?

The Zoology was edited by Darwin and included five parts, each authored by an expert in a particular field: Richard Owen for <u>Fossil Mammalia</u>, George Robert

Waterhouse for <u>Mammalia</u>, John Gould for <u>Birds</u>, Leonard Jenyns for <u>Fish</u>, and Thomas Bell for <u>Reptiles</u>. While Darwin and his colleagues came out of a tradition of naturalist-artists, among the authors of *The Zoology*, only John Gould made his own drawings and paintings. Who made all of those other extraordinary illustrations?

I have been poring over the Darwin Online web site, where virtually every page of every Darwin notebook, manuscript and published work has been scanned and cataloged. There is little credit given to the artists and lithographers who portrayed the physical evidence of Darwin's claim. In some cases, their names appear on the plates, along with those of printers and publishers. The 32 plates in Part I of *The Zoology* are inscribed, "G. Scharf del et lithog [drawing and lithography]." But Scharf is not credited on the title page of the volume or even with the List of Plates.

Now consider the descriptive text by Richard Owen for the *Toxodon platensis* of Plate I, and how helpful it would be to have Scharf's drawing at hand: "The general form of the skull, as seen from above, is pyriform; but viewed sideways, and without the lower jaw, it is semi-ovate; it is depressed, elongate, of considerable breadth, including the span of the zygomatic arches, but becoming rather suddenly contracted anterior to them, the facial part thence growing narrower to near the muzzle, which again slightly expands. . . . " And it goes on.

It seems to me that we owe some acknowledgment to those who documented the fossil record and the living record, and conveyed graphically the fundamentals of evolution before the age of digital technology. The lithographers named were often working from the sketches made by other artists. At least G. Scharf, being both artist and lithographer, lives on alongside Darwin's legacy. In some respects, Scharf himself was a scientist. He received his training at the Royal Academy of Arts and Sciences in Munich; and the form of printmaking he practiced, lithography, was the new high-tech process of his day. But what I learned of his career saddened me.

George Johann Scharf (1788–1860) completed his schooling in 1810 and traveled Europe in search of commissions. In 1816 he settled in London, where throughout his life he made sketches and watercolors of the city. His primary source of employment was illustration and lithography, but his commission from Charles Darwin proved to be the beginning of his professional decline. Darwin felt that Scharf's price for a series of illustrations of fossil bones from South America was too high. The men had a falling out, after which the artist's commissions began to dry up. Scharf spent his last years struggling to sell his work with little success. But after his death, his wife sold more than a thousand pieces to the British Museum. Accurate, beautiful and evocative, Scharf's paintings and sketches provide a vivid portrait of Victorian London before the invention of photography.

I looked in vain for any decent drawing made by Darwin. He may have been an intellectual giant, but he needed his illustrators. Their visual record remains direct and universal, preserving the sense of his research and his times. In many ways, those drawings have drawn him for us, showing us the world through his eyes as he sought out significant details in organic forms. It is here, in the passionate, probing observation of nature that Science and Art overlap.

Reality Check
March 2013

I've been writing a lot about the extreme amount of violence in our culture. There are 60-second movie trailers on TV that make me feel like I've been through a war, they are so full of noisy, bloody mayhem. So we had a bit of a reality check the other night when we tuned in to a nature documentary about how animals survive a long northern winter. This particular study involved bison and wolves.

Brilliant photography brought us every aspect of their movements and activities. Much of it was shot from above as these animals moved across vast landscapes. We hadn't been watching long when the scene got very tense. A herd of bison was traveling in a tight knot with their young in the center of it, and a pack of wolves was literally dogging their heels—charging into them, nipping, taking great chances amid the hoofs of those many-times-larger beasts with horns.

We had seen the wolf pups frolicking earlier. As with the buffalo and their young, the familial scene

126

immediately evoked empathy, a sense of relatedness to that protective feeling of the adult for the young, and delight in the adorable play of the little ones. Now, as the wolves flat out attacked the bison with strategic, single-minded prowess, it became ever more clear that they would not give up until they had taken down the young prey. They had their own brood to feed. As if they too understood the universality of parental feeling, they charged the herd with ferocity and managed to split it. The knot of bison, made smaller by two, hurried ahead to save what they could. A single adult bison was left to fend off a pack of five large wolves. It fought valiantly, but when it became clear that the baby bison would not get away, we quickly changed the channel— we who can sit through apocalyptic destruction of whole cities with a yawn.

Nature is cruel. Life is prolific and for the most part short lived. Lots of life and lots of death. And you can't pretend that the animals don't feel this, that we're the only ones. The bison will miss its babe. The wolf will run itself near to death to feed its pup. Science has only begun to explore the self- and social awareness of other species, and how that may relate to that of humans.

Conversely, we know humans also have a survival instinct that can drive one to kill in order to live. This mechanism demands a distinguishing of "us" from "them," which in modern humans is mostly conceptual. A curious species surveilling us from above would not see anything so different in our warring armies as wolves and bison. And peering into our domiciles, they may find us well stocked and nowhere near the dire straits of a wolf in winter. Yet we still fight each other.

The wolf and the bison got me thinking about the old concept of Zion that I learned in Sunday School. "Where the lamb will lie down with the lion." It was not a conception of any place on this earth, to be sure. To attain Zion we literally have to go to another plane of existence, where the laws of nature do not demand that the lion eat the lamb or perish. To date, prayers and dutiful observance of ritual have not succeeded in taking us there. Even if all humans obeyed the same moral/civil law, and we miraculously achieved peace among ourselves, the lion and the wolf would still have to eat—and so would we.

Non-theists like to point to all of the violence, injustice and sorrow in the world as evidence that there is no King of Peace running the show here. Nature is all there is. But nature, if not consciously cruel, is destructive, insatiable, relentless. Religions have visualized more perfect worlds in which we are freed from nature. Since humanists don't buy that, we are challenged to find other responses to the harshness of nature and the pain of existence.

My answer is Art. What's yours?

The Circle Way
May 2013

Humanists hold a naturalistic philosophy versus a supernatural belief, meaning we dispense with gods and religious doctrine. The roots of secular humanism grow out of and in reaction to the Judeo-Christian religions, and we still tend to explain ourselves in the context of our opposition to what I call the He-god of the Old Testament and the Christian Bible.

What we *are* is *not that*. Not authoritarian, not patriarchal, not superstitious, not seeking salvation in an afterlife, not accepting myth as history or ancient texts as revealed wisdom that supercedes direct experience and observation. Humanism is post-religion, an innovation in consciousness, social organization and problem solving that has been developing for many centuries and is gradually coming to predominate modern thought.

Where things get dicey is this concept of "spirit"—not a god spirit but our own. Something is alive within us. If we acknowledge that we are part of nature and subject to its laws, then that spark or spirit as we perceive it must be part of other living things as well. Religions have claimed certain traits exclusively for humankind as imbued by a creator, but science is finding more and more of these traits in other species: play, decorative art, the concept of fairness, tool use and language, to name a few. Science has allowed us to cast off the theistic notion of human superiority (below God but above Nature) in favor of placing us squarely within this marvelous system of unknown and possibly unknowable origin. The resulting sense of wonder, curiosity and aliveness is, for many of us, close if not equivalent to a spiritual feeling. But the word "spirit" still rankles—we wouldn't want to be misconstrued as holding an irrational belief in something outside of our physical existence!

Be that as it may, the spirit is strong in New Mexico. We live alongside indigenous peoples whose philosophy and traditions are far removed from those of our puritanical predecessors. If we put aside our antagonism for anything religious or ritualistic, we might recognize a form of humanism and kindred naturalistic attitudes that can help us reconcile science and spirit.

My friend Stephen Sachs, a PhD in Political Science, has written an unabashedly spiritual book of commentary and poem-prayers. *Walking The Four Directions* (Eagle Spirit Publishing, 2011) is based on his participation in many Native American ceremonies. In the wake of several mass killings this spring, from intentional slaughter to industrial accident, I was struck by this passage, which refers to the circle in ceremony, and as an organizing social principle:

"Reverence for all of nature, of which people are a part, guides the behavior expected within community, which is primary to one's identity. In general each individual seeing him/herself in relationship to all others in the community feels a responsibility to act properly and cooperatively, to maintain a harmonious and balanced set of relationships. Everyone affected by a decision must have a say in its making, for places in the circle have no meaning without the whole of the circle. Likewise there is no circle without each of the individual locations, with their unique way of seeing and contributing to the whole. "

This is at once a spiritual and rational stance. In our modern society, we can be technologically networked to the world, yet actually quite isolated. When too many are left out of the circle, disruption and destruction ensue. The Native American concepts of balance, beauty and community strike a strong chord with me, as I find myself more often describing my philosophy as naturalistic rather than nontheist or agnostic. It puts me in the circle instead of outside of it. The circle is not only the blessing way and the beauty way, it is the humanist way.

Conflict of Interest
September 2013

The pair of Cooper's hawks that nests in the fringe of trees lining the irrigation ditch has been quite visible this past month. I have delighted to see them maneuvering through the treetops with strands of dried grass and vine for their nest, or flying low in a zig-zag pattern over the ditch to flush out prey. I startled one out of the brush grasping a fresh kill in its talons, and I saw one up in the cottonwood tearing into its meal and then cleaning its beak on the rough tree bark. The dogs are well aware of the discards of the hawks' kills, and occasionally the hawks themselves leave a feather behind for me to wear in the band of my straw hat.

Sometimes a hawk will pay me a call. The hawk perches on the cable over the back alley, and we get a good look at each other out from under cover of the trees. But it is disconcerting to have the predator lurking around my own turf.

There is a pair of thrashers living in the walking stick cactus at the back of our property. We (humans, dogs, thrashers) have grown used to each other. One evening I got to see three baby thrashers pop out of their hiding places and perch on the tips of the cactus, waiting for their parents to bring them bugs. Over the next week, I watched the chicks practice hopping from the cactus to the back wall, then flutter up into a nearby tree. Soon they were following their parents around the yard. The hawk started showing up late morning hoping to catch one unawares.

"Oh no you don't!" I told the hawk, whom I had watched for eagerly not half an hour before and just half a block away. "Go hunt somewhere else!" I paced around the cactus protectively while the thrasher shrieked. (An adult thrasher will sound the alarm to get everyone back into the cactus, and then keep shrieking as long as the hawk is perched overhead.) The hawk reluctantly gave up and glided slowly northward, hunting. The thrasher popped out of the cactus, and we stood companionably watching the sky for several minutes to be sure the hawk wouldn't circle back.

The hawks have their own demanding young to feed. I have seen them too. And I wonder if my sentimentality has subverted some precise, passionless law of nature, such as: for every three baby thrashers born, one must be taken by a hawk. And if such a rule exists, are the hawks themselves aware of it? If the hawk were to snag one of our thrasher babies, would it move on to another nest? More likely, wouldn't it come right back and try to repeat its success? I'm not sure that the hawk has a sense of fairness, or that the thrasher would be philosophical about the loss of even one chick.

One can get into trouble ascribing human feelings and reasoning to other species. But we can learn quite a lot from watching the variety and interplay of life around us, as well as our reactions to it. Fairy tales and fables feature much interaction between people and animals, and often the transformation of one type of creature into another. The animals and plants, with their characteristic traits, provide metaphors for all of the internal, inter-personal and practical conflicts that plague the human mind. The imagery of the plant and animal kingdoms surely preceded language, and is still pervasive in our thoughts whether or not we live in close proximity to nature. While there are many environmental reasons to protect the diversity of species and prevent extinctions, I think that our inner lives would also be far poorer without the wild things.

The Compassion Gap
October 2013

Here are some items that have come to my attention lately that speak to the growing economic inequality in the U.S., an issue humanists should be concerned about, and that we are in a unique position to address—if we have the courage to do so.

* *All Things Considered* (National Public Radio), 8/8/10, "Study: Poor Are More Charitable Than The Wealthy." Guy Raz interviewed psychology researcher Paul Piff, whose game-playing subjects received ten credits (in lieu of cash) and determined how many, if any, would be given to a partner that was a stranger to them. "[W]hat we found was that the lower-class people . . . were inclined to give away forty-four percent more [of their credits]," Piff reported. "[I]t's really compassionate feelings that exist among the lower class that's seen to provoke these higher levels of altruism and generosity toward other people."

* *Money News*, 9/13/13, "Krugman: Growing Inequality is Becoming Extremely Destructive" by Michael King. King quotes Krugman: "Inherited privilege is crowding out equality of opportunity; the power of money is crowding out effective democracy," and cites these numbers: "95 percent of the gains from economic recovery since 2009 have gone to the top 1 percent. . . . more than 60 percent of the gains went to

the top 0.1 percent, people with annual incomes of more than 1.9 million."

* *Albuquerque Journal*, 9/19/13, "Census: N.M. poverty rate increased from 2000 to 2012" by Barry Massey. The article notes that 43 other states have seen the same trend.

* CNN, 9/21/13, "House bill would take 3.8 million off food stamps" by Jennifer Liberto. The legislation would cut $40 billion over the next decade.

Some might accuse me of engaging in "class warfare" for simply citing these items. If the term applies at all, then who is making war on whom? It seems like the rich are making war on the poor, not the other way around. But the moneyed interests cry foul whenever we bring up income disparities and ask that wealth be shared for the good of all. I guess it hurts the billionaires' feelings when we peons dare to suggest that no one is deserving of the kind of personal income that rivals the budgets of small countries.

Call it what you will, there seems to be a compassion gap every bit as wide as the financial divide. Humanists would do well to engage this debate. We reject out of hand the underlying puritanical mindset by which greed is rationalized as merely holding on to what was divinely granted, and suffering is either a hallowed martyrdom or something actually deserved. Further, we embrace scientific method and critical thinking, through which we can put aside emotions and assumptions in order to collect measurable data and compare results objectively. By objective standards of prosperity such as mortality rates, education and employment, the U.S. is falling behind. That should tell us something about our brand of capitalism.

We humanists have our own blind spots and self-interests. Shall we reject the supernatural gods only to embrace without question the equally broad concept of money? If you feel I have blasphemed in the way I phrased that, then I've made my point. Money is a kind of god, and capitalism is its religion. I propose that a society where some people starve while others get millions of dollars per year from businesses that deplete and despoil their nation's natural resources has severed its connection to reality every bit as much as a society ruled by superstition and religious dogma.

"Non-participation is itself a form of dissent," a wise friend once told me. We see an example of this in the *Albuquerque Journal*, 9/19/13 Letter to the Editor, "Radical simple living is good for me and the earth" by Don Schrader. Don describes his satisfaction with his drastically scaled-down lifestyle. He does not paint himself a martyr or judge the rest of us, but closes simply with this advice: "Change as fast as you can as long as you enjoy it and are quite sure you will stick with it for life."

Few of us are as brave or committed or contrary or crazy—or whatever you want to call it—as Don Schrader. We see the need all around us, and we aspire to increased prosperity as much for others as ourselves. The question in my mind is this: Can fairness, equality and security ever be attained under our existing economic construct, or are we stuck in a game in which there will always be—there must be—lots and lots of losers in order that a few will win big? If the latter, then we are going down the path of many a fallen empire.

A Kind of Hope
November 2013

Someone special died. I know that everyone is special to somebody, or to a few or many others. But I write of someone who wasn't a close personal friend of mine—she was someone I knew, and she was special. We all know people like that. They shine. They uplift by their very presence. Here was a woman beautiful inside and out, talented and hardworking, smart and generous. I know there must have been times when she didn't smile, but I never witnessed any. She was in the middle of life and full of life, even in the face of a cancer that had taken the lives of close family members and would eventually take hers.

Nature's pretty sneaky with those genes. The science of it can leave one feeling powerless or alienated. If we are each just a cocktail of chemicals that's been cooked up in a long series of unsupervised experiments to no particular purpose, then what is the point of—anything? It would not be unreasonable to drift from this existential dilemma into nihilism, and submerge oneself in an indulgent lifestyle of excess and excitement—even, or especially, if that meant hastening the inevitable end. Yet

I have never known anyone who was facing impending death who did that. Yes, they reprioritized, but the principles and the people they cared about didn't drop down on the list just because chemistry had decreed the situation to be hopeless.

Throughout our lives we experience events that are hard to accept, impossible to undo, painful to remember. Reinterpreting such events with a spiritual spin or in a mythic context can be a healing practice. Meditation, dream-work, therapy and prayer have proven to be effective techniques for dealing with sudden change and misfortune. But I draw the line at looking for any kind of moral or karmic "reason" for a jumble of events in which I and mine are mere, fleeting specks. For me, the superficially random but actually quite consistent processes of nature offer more comfort in trying times than the idea that we have arrived at this place by some willful action of an outside force. Or willful inaction. (If such a force exists, it is appalling indeed—I don't see how I could possibly appease it even if I tried.)

I was asked recently, following a talk I gave about humanism, where I find hope in the absence of religious faith and belief in god. "In humanity?" the questioner guessed with a hint of disapproval in his voice.

"Well, yes, in humanity," I told him. "But what I was going to say is that I find my hope in the fact that humans don't have all the answers, that we're capable of learning more and being better, and figuring out how to solve our problems and live together. I know it's easy to look around at today's society and say, 'Not much hope here,' but my hope, my belief, is that it isn't going to be this way forever. This is not all there is, this is not the best we can be. We can and will continue to evolve."

Well, there were no more questions after that! But many questions remain for me and for humanists. Looking for the answers is what pushes us forward and keeps things interesting. Our curiosity is a kind of hope. As for comfort, our minds and imaginations allow us to transform intense emotional experiences into a story that does have meaning as it threads its way through all the highs and lows of life. I suppose that's why I write—so that I can start out with a lament, "Someone special died," and work my way around to, "Someone special lived, and I was lucky to know her."

But I'm still p.o.'d at those stupid genes.

Come as You Are
February 2014

Here is something rather simple that I especially treasure about our humanist community: I feel that in your company I can be myself and say what I think, and I can trust you to do the same. Honesty and trust—it doesn't get much better than that.

When humanists converse among ourselves, our ideas may be accepted, rejected or corrected, but our responses to each other do not come as a judgment from on high or filtered through a set of entrenched expectations. We connect to each other directly. The language we speak is grounded in the everyday and the evident—documented history, verifiable facts, knowledge of natural processes, and the empathy of one confused, imperfect mortal for another.

One need not repeat a series of secret knocks to be admitted to the humanist circle. Arcane initiations are not required. Our values and ethics spring from our awareness that humans, however varied, are more alike than different, and that humanity is inextricably connected to nature. Our shared belief, grounded in experience, is that some things are knowable, and human knowledge serves humanity and the planet better than human ignorance.

Humanist philosophy asserts that people have a natural inclination to fairness and morality. Without the promise of heaven or the threat of hell, we will still strive to behave ethically. Examples of this abound in our humanist communities, where our good works are motivated by sincere respect and regard for each other. In my humanist dream, everyone has a chance to fulfill their own unique potential, so that we may attain a sustainable and peaceful society through embracing diversity and fostering creativity.

Certainly the higher ideals of humankind have not so far been achieved through authoritarian insistence on conformity to an imposed order. To the contrary, attempts to constrain the human imagination and redirect communal energy by brute or psychological force only breed frustration, strife and resistance. Too often, those who are vested with "spiritual" authority are actually focused on reining in the vitality of the human spirit.

What I have observed of religious belief, practice, and community is that there is always a point at which one is asked to repress one's own (choose all that apply): instincts, individuality, opinion, questions, knowledge, direct experience, desire. Apparently, piety can only be measured in terms of the difficulty of overcoming a natural or automatic inclination. We are presented with a series of tests in which the object of the game is actually to be *not* oneself, but a magically better being for having suppressed personal perspective and submitted to the group myth. Efforts to draw back the curtain, assertive skepticism, any perceived subversion of traditional practice are threatening and unwelcome. In other words, "faking it" is rewarded, or at least smooths the way, whereas honesty becomes problematic.

I did not realize, until I had spent some time in the humanist community, how often I censored myself, even in conversation with good friends. Smile and nod, smile and nod. I would never dare to challenge someone's taste, and certainly not their beliefs. But why should I not express my own? Thanks to our freethought community, I do express my thoughts more freely. It's not so much a matter of being more courageous as simply being more in practice.

It is important to have an intellectual home, a setting in which to fully and freely exercise our minds. Our humanist societies have had no trouble filling this need. But humanism encompasses every aspect of human existence, and our organizations face many challenges when it comes to addressing the emotional and practical needs of our members. The question arises: Can we provide a home for the heart as well?

Metaphors Work for Me
March 2014

Is solace only possible through the suspension of disbelief? This question has been rattling around in my mind lately. To put it more bluntly: Do I really have to "drink the cool-aid" to gain peace of mind?

Peace of mind, solace, forgiveness, courage—these are emotional needs that spiritual and religious practices set out to fill. Those of us raised in the Judeo-Christian tradition perhaps noticed that the same beliefs intended to provide inner strength were also effective at feeding guilt and insecurity—necessitating more solace, comfort, etc. We suspected it was all intended to keep us busy and obedient with manufactured needs and misdirected fears. Our first step in actually finding peace of mind, then, would be to purge our minds of those oppressive myths and imaginary threats.

"I am done with the judging, vindictive god." Really, I had that figured out by the time I was ten. But it doesn't change the fact of those first impressionable years, and so I have been judging myself ever since. Peace of mind remains elusive. Still, a first step is a first step. And shrugging off the patronizing, puritanical, tyrannical weight of an organized religion was a huge first step for me.

Where do we go from there? Many in my generation—and I suspect this is still true today—looked out
across the religious landscape and wondered what we
were missing. We were ready to give up a religion, but
not all religion. Some looked for a better match in
Eastern, Pagan, or Indigenous traditions. Since these
have their own imposed rigors of behavior and ritual
practice, others preferred the New Age buffet of
mix-'n-match rites from any and every "spiritual"
source. "Spiritual" was preferred over "religious" so as
to distinguish between an organizational structure and
something pure, personal, internal.

What about that peace of mind? I know that many
people who leave the religion they were raised in do find
a home in another faith community, whether traditional,
adapted or invented. I'll go further and say that in the
whole gamut of spiritual practices and philosophies we
will find a lot of overlap with humanism. It is one of our
own tenets, after all, that morality and compassion are
natural human traits—we would expect to find similar
humanitarian concerns, for instance, across the religious
to nonreligious spectrum. Where we do not overlap is in
the acceptance of a central myth as truth. Humanists do
not endorse belief in myths no matter how benign,
creative or comforting they may be.

I wonder why the metaphor itself can't be enough.
Those myths are not going away any time soon. The
gods, the saints, Adam and Eve, the damn snake, Noah,
Shiva, Zeus—they are part of our history, language and

collective imagination. You could say we're stuck with them, but why let them be a burden? Stories—our ability to invent them, adjust them and interpret them—are an essential element of human existence. To accept a story *as a story*—so that it can be examined, discussed, even re-imagined as starting, progressing and culminating in a variety of ways—enhances our understanding of ourselves and the world.

Passive faith in the story as truth, on the other hand, can be truly destructive. If we can't distinguish between actual history and the stories we make up, then how will we ever confront the future, and the impact that our behavior (not beliefs!) will have on human destiny?

Faith traditions profess to offer serenity, hope and joy to the true believer. We can debate whether that is typically the case, but my interest here is in whether we can have all of those good feelings without the supernatural belief. As far as I can tell, humanists are a happy bunch—also brave, caring and optimistic. The ills of the world—poverty, violence, injustice—present themselves to us not as punishments, lessons or karmic score keeping to be reconciled emotionally and then "let go," but as conditions that require and are capable of correction—by people!

My conclusion is that facing reality isn't a hindrance to peace of mind, and solace comes from confronting problems honestly in the knowledge that we are equipped and empowered to work toward solutions.

Renaissance 2.1
May 2014

I'm glad that the new *Cosmos* series is airing two nights a week, because sometimes it takes two viewings to see it all. I confess, I am apt to nod off during any program about astronomy. Once the screen is filled with the night sky, and we start zooming through outer space, my mind begins to drift into space as well. We are traveling at the speed of light . . . tracing the universe back in time . . . approaching the Big Bang . . . entering a Black Hole. . . .

I almost dozed off just thinking about it. Black Holes do it every time, not to mention quarks, dark matter, neutrinos—I have been known to fall asleep during the opening credits. To be fair, programs on paleontology and biology can have the same effect, and once the double helix shows up, and a narrator starts breaking down the components of DNA— Good night, nurse!

I'm doing better with the new *Cosmos*, which benefits greatly from advances in digital production. There is nothing the artists cannot do in the way of animation, and the writers and directors are adept at using their skills to keep my attention on the screen.

Maybe you've noticed how the current series uses high-tech visualizations to convey abstract concepts and phenomena beyond natural human perception, but turns to fairly rudimentary animations to depict the historical events surrounding scientific discoveries. When a story is of a human scale, we don't need all those bells and whistles to keep us tuned in—our own experience allows us to mentally flesh out the characters, even their inner emotions, from a graphically flat, almost abstracted presentation.

By approaching its topics from a variety of angles and points of view, *Cosmos* keeps my attention from flying into space and drifting off into dreamland. The episodes jump around a bit much—from the Big Bang to life in a dew drop—but I can't complain. Those conceptual leaps and directorial cuts have kept me not only awake but actively processing the wide-ranging and complex material.

One of the great challenges of science is achieving objectivity. What is true, has been true, and will remain true, regardless of human perception and consciousness? Since we only know the world through our minds and living experience, we must engage in elaborate mental gymnastics to imagine ourselves outside of humanity, to think through what reality is on the macro scale of the entire cosmos, and the micro scale of genes and atoms. Mathematics, at once relentlessly precise and utterly abstract, provides a specialized language through which to deal objectively with our explorations of the world.

The challenge of teaching science and math also involves subjectivity. We must make all of that objective knowledge meaningful to the students, so they will be motivated to learn. But desire alone isn't enough. New information sticks better if it can be attached to some relevant existing knowledge or familiar activity. The simple act of drawing or viewing a picture can be sufficient to make that connection. Biographies of people who figured out how things work create an emotional connection and provide a common narrative context—the life story—which brings otherwise remote matters into focus.

The arts and sciences have always been inextricably linked. What I find so exciting about art and science in the digital age is that the correlation of the two has come so close as to actually eliminate, in many cases, that old fudge factor we used to call "artistic license." The artists and animators of today's science programs can readily translate a point to a pixel to produce an absolutely accurate graphic representation of how and where and when particles, cells, people and planets exist. They may use the very same tools that the scientists use—the same tools that we ourselves may have available on our home computers and even our phones.

Cosmos demonstrates the heights to which our digital age can take us. The series' exceptional integration of disciplines points to a potential coming Renaissance for the 21st century, in which human knowledge and artistic expression will again surge forward in tandem. I hope I'm not just dreaming.

The Songs of Unseen Birds
June 2014

I walk in the cool of the morning, and the air around me is alive with bird calls. I stop and look up into the trees. All the young foliage is moving lightly in the breeze and glimmering in the dappled sunlight. I cannot locate a single bird, in flight or otherwise. My ears direct my eyes to look—over there, up here, right behind me, right above me.... I recognize the melodious calls of robins, the squealing of hummingbirds, cooing of doves, the twittering of the LBJs ("little brown jobs"), and a pair of blackbirds laughing back and forth. Obviously I am surrounded by birds, but my bedazzled eyes cannot make out even one.

At other times, the trail is silent, unnaturally so. The birds are keeping quiet on purpose—"not a peep," as they say. I conclude that the hawks must be hunting. I start looking and listening for them. I expect to see or hear them soon, and I often do. This gets me thinking about how many years I walked these trails, and others, and never thought much about the hidden world existing right above me in the trees. It has always been there, and there have always been people who enjoyed closely observing it. Over time, I have become one of them.

I might use the obviously present but generally invisible birds in the treetops as a metaphor for all of the components that make up the universe. Observant people have long understood that everything is made of something, moved by something. They supposed the existence of particles, waves, fields, and the like. Their conviction that physical reality could not exist as it does without such an understructure drove them to invent techniques for revealing and measuring things that are not obvious to our senses. Along the way, they had to endure a lot of scoffers. Even today, there are religious fundamentalists for whom accepted scientific discoveries about the makeup and history of the world are still unproved conjecture. They can hear the birdcalls, but refuse to make the logical leap, or even to accept the testimony of someone who has climbed the tree.

Strangely, my metaphor can be applied equally well to describe ideas that seem antithetical to science. Imagine that the twittering in the treetops represents another kind of hidden world that exists within reach of our comprehension, but is generally imperceptible. Call that world Spirit. Awareness of it can come gradually or suddenly. People might go for long periods or their whole lives without perceiving it or looking for it. Meditation, like a walk in the woods, can bring one to the quiet, patient place where this wondrous world can be detected.

Like the songs of unseen birds, there are certain sensations that one may perceive and then process into the conclusion: There must be something here. I refer to dreams and daydreams, deja vu, serendipitous or coincidental encounters that feel fateful, worries that prove prescient, impulses that verge on telepathic, and strokes of artistic inspiration. Shall we naturalists, in the name of reason, reject the input from our own bodies? Reason tells me that although there is no evidence for an outside, sentient, supernatural force that creates these phenomena for its own purpose, the phenomena exist nonetheless, so there must be a source, and a natural system in which they operate. If we are creative and persistent enough, we may find ways to discover more about these experiences.

Psychology and cognitive science are already unlocking many secrets of our mental and emotional functions. Perhaps this realm is also made up of particles, fields and waves that will one day prove to be the source of magical-seeming mental transmissions and ideas. Maybe it all does boil down to chemistry. But we should be humble in our assumptions about our capacity to objectively examine and accurately perceive the structure of our own consciousness. How many more layers of reality do exist to which we have not yet gained access?

Now I'm wondering why I have risked my good humanist reputation to speculate on such things as spirit, telepathy and precognition. I guess because a little birdie told me.

Go Out and Be Awesome
July 2014

I want to try to write down my "elevator speech" from the recent AHA National Conference in Philadelphia, where I led and represented the AHA Feminist Caucus at several activities.

I was approached by dedicated humanists of all ages with many questions and ideas for the feminist movement. Their earnestness convinced me that with such a strong desire for institutional change, and such actual, dramatic change on an interpersonal level when it comes to gender identity and equality, we must surely be poised to prevail. Strident opposition to the mere word "feminism" has started to sound more like the howl of a dying beast than a battle cry. Maybe there's less fight in the champions of the status quo than we imagine. With this in mind, my own call to arms, such as it was, came out something like this:

Not everyone is an activist. We get involved because we have to—we see something that is wrong and we jump in. There are people who are good at activism and enjoy it and make a career or ongoing project of it, but that's not for all of us, and it shouldn't be. If our desire is to live in a free and fair society where we can all pursue our unique interests and fulfill our unique potential, then activism, for most of us, cannot be an end in itself. If a goal of feminism is to have more women achieving more opportunities and positions of influence in all walks of life, then we have to set our sights beyond the next cause, and tend to our own careers and self-actualization.

Yes, there is a lot that needs doing in the feminist-humanist movement, and a lot to be gained from getting involved and learning organizational and leadership skills. There are serious injustices to rectify, and we all have a part to play in mobilizing against discrimination. But I think that all of our humanist organizations need to focus more on helping and urging women and men to get down to our own work, to valuing and cultivating our unique interests and skills, to becoming accomplished and successful in whatever we do, so that we will be influential by virtue of the examples we set. This is where we truly make our mark on the world, in our daily living and interactions.

I am an artist, writer and publisher. I feel that when I do these things well I am helping humanity, not letting humanity down because I didn't do other things. I'm lucky to live at a time when I can pursue such endeavors and even aspire to achieve recognition for my work— without having to change my name to George. It would be ironic to divert all of my energy to organizing for equal rights while neglecting to "do my own thing."

I'm an activist because I have to be, because I see my sisters and brothers in the fight, and I want to share the load with them. But I owe it to the ones who came before me to seize the opportunities they didn't have, to assert an identity unique and of my own choosing. And that is what I want for everyone.

It concerns me to see people, especially women, simply shifting from one kind of self-sacrifice to another, or from traditional domestic roles to modern but equally constricting social projects.

Cooperation toward a worthy goal should not mean submission or regimentation. That's why, to all the wonderful people who want to know, *What can I do? What more can I do?* for the feminist-humanist cause, the best I can recommend is this: Go out and be awesome.

Childhood
September 2014

We all survive our childhoods. Obviously, or we wouldn't be here. But we do not come through unmarked. The innocence of childhood is much overplayed. Children catch on pretty quickly to both blatant and subtle signals coming from those around them. Adults' embarrassment, worry, amusement, satisfaction, confusion and dishonesty are all registered if not fully understood by humans of very young age.

Childhood by its nature is full of firsts. Novel experiences can stay with us forever. We hope these will be encouraging, educational, beneficial memories. Since Frank and I have been caring for a stray cat and her kittens this summer, I have been recalling being a kid, and the time our pet cat gave birth to her litter in the middle of the night. That was an eye-opener, to say the least. We had gotten a paperback book about cat care and prepared for the event. The mother cat had not read the book, but everything proceeded without too much fuss, naturally.

I know we had the kittens long enough to give them names—all literary women: Emily and Charlotte Bronte, Agatha Christie and Daphne DuMaurier, though as it turned out, they were not all female. We kept "Daffy." Dad took the others to the SPCA. His earlier jokes about rocks and sacks and rivers hadn't gone over real well. I remember having the uneasy feeling that my father, in other circumstances, could have and would have dispatched the newborn kittens. He'd been to war, after all. But it turned out he was no match for three daughters, a wife, and mother-in-law.

Memories of recurring events become embedded through repetition. It is hard to remember the very first experience of an annual family tradition. Details change from year to year, but the format is the same. An iconic memory emerges; here's one of mine:

Every Mother's Day we'd pile into the station wagon—my Mom and Dad, myself and my two sisters, Grandma Sarah, Aunt Sarah, and sometimes Grandma Sadie and Grandpa Julie—and drive to Bordentown, New Jersey, which was exactly halfway between our home in Wilmington, Delaware and Uncle Irv's house in Teaneck. There was a Howard Johnson's at the Bordentown exit of the NJ Turnpike, where Irv, Aunt Gladys and cousin Howie would meet us. It always rained (that's how I remember it) so that after our big lunch, we'd rush out to the station wagon and squeeze everyone in to give the Mother's Day gifts; and although Aunt Sarah wasn't married and wasn't a mom, she too got gifts. It was a happy time, all crowded in together, the rain beating down. Often the sun would come out, finally, about the time we were ready to head home.

How idyllic it all sounds. But even my safely swaddled suburban upbringing was edged with heartache, and rumbled with undertones of old family feuds. Worse was Hebrew School and the history lessons concerning attacks on Jews in the Holocaust, the Russian pogroms, the Spanish Inquisition, and all the way back to biblical times. Not the best fodder for a young, extremely vivid imagination. When I was older and attempting an objective assessment of my roots, I would look back on all of that as amounting to a form of abuse, though it probably didn't seem so to the more extroverted or inattentive or tough-minded kids.

I wonder what it would be like to have grown up without having to look so deeply, so early, into the darkest aspects of human experience—to have ever been innocent. I will never know. Still, I only had to experience those violations of humanity in my imagination, intellectually, emotionally. How much more branded, if not stunted, is the person who really suffered such things, who has survived physically but must live with the scars and trauma.

People do come through and overcome the most horrendous deprivation and assaults. We console ourselves with uplifting examples of those who are "now living a normal life" and the knowledge that at least some are able to put the past behind them and enjoy a secure and fulfilled adulthood.

Yes, humans are resilient. We who are here are all survivors. But there can be no reclaiming the time when a healthy new mind is poised on the brink of awareness and prepared to burst into willful, curious, joyful discovery. That is a moment of potentiality that only comes once in a lifetime.

Imagine the beauty and achievements of a society in which all children have that moment of innocence, that sense of security, that chance to thrive. Imagine a world in which we do more than survive.

Prophets vs. Profits
October 2014

It's not easy being a prophet. I can see why those guys were all so grumpy. Here you've seen the future plain as day in a dream or waking vision—you know disaster is looming, but with this fortuitous advance warning the worst can be avoided—only, no one will listen. The biblical prophets were mainly treated with derision in their own time, and their stories come down to us as tales of seeming crazy people who spoke to God or were visited by angels or otherwise saw signs and wonders. Some were vindicated when the events they foretold came to pass. However, the way the stories get spun is that God is the one who is vindicated, because He was the one whispering into the ear of the prophet.

Putting aside their legendary dreams and visions, it's quite possible the prophets were just smart people who could see a little further than the ends of their noses. They may have been observant, critical thinkers capable of working out causal relationships, and willing to venture an educated guess about how to avoid a bad situation in the future or rectify an existing one.

The problem with being a prophet—versus, say, a saint or angel or messiah—is that you are all too human and usually long-lived. So, you get to 1) be mocked and 2) suffer the dire events you had tried to prevent and, worst of all, 3) listen to everyone whine about it. "I told you so" is no consolation at all; and if your doomsaying made you the object of disdain in the past, rubbing it in that you were right may get you pilloried.

The prophets of legend were all too human and were probably humanists. Perhaps the dreams and visions, signs and wonders were only fictions designed to galvanize action using the vernacular of the day. I bet we have a lot of scientists, educators, doctors, farmers, artists and accountants who feel like modern day prophets as they watch the future unfold.

We talked about the dangers of global malnutrition forty years ago; today not only is hunger rampant around the globe but increasingly here in the U.S. as well. For decades now, experts have been telling us about the dangers of industrial pollution, nuclear waste, mega-farming, infrastructure decline, the military-industrial complex and endless war, gun violence, copyright abuse, surveillance and tracking by government and private industry, and deteriorating educational and health standards, among many other woes of the twenty-first century. Unfortunately, these experts don't get a lot of media bookings. Preference is given to political pundits, who enact a dialogue (at best) or dramatic disagreement that is a lot like theater, so that even as viewer emotions are heightened, our sense of reality is diminished, and with it the idea that we should or could take action.

The tools of divination are all around us—the very test of sound science is its ability to predict using procedures that can be duplicated and relied on to yield consistent results. Apocalyptic warnings from contemporary prophets are truly distressing exactly because they are founded in verifiable facts, not take-my-word-for-it visions. But we have good reason to believe that solutions are also within our power, assuming we can get our heads out of the clouds, or out of the sand.

Part 4

We All Deserve Better

Selected Essays from
"The Tree" blog
May 2013 – September 2016

I Wouldn't Want to Be a Guy
May 22, 2013

So I had a root canal and it hurt like hell. Which got me thinking about what it must feel like to be punched in the jaw. Which got me thinking about what it must be like to be a guy—to be expected to "take it on the chin" and otherwise be prepared for rough if not violent physical engagement.

If you think about the dual roles men are expected to play in society, you'll find they are every bit as unrealistic and incompatible as the roles foisted on women. While women teeter crazily between playing household drudge and sex goddess, the male balancing act involves having to be rough and tumble on the one hand and suave and savvy on the other.

At the end of a typical day in our imaginary Camelot of gender perfection, the wife discards her housecoat and do-rag and slips into a tight little something that is decidedly less comfortable. Her husband, having spent the day in his unnaturally groomed, socially acceptable persona, returns home to exchange his business suit for shorts and t-shirt, indulge his beard stubble for a few precious hours, and tend to manly shlepping and fixing projects. Or he might just plop down on the couch to release his pent-up macho watching sports or action

161

fliks. In either case, presumably, the woman's extra-feminine elaboration combined with her man's stripped-down masculinity combine into the happy super-completeness of heterosexual mating.

Have I described a bygone age, stereotypes that only linger in old movies and sitcoms? If so, that is only because the middle class is on its way out, and with it the traditional male-female division of labor which virtually defined the middle class we boomers were born into. Everyone had a job to do, and did it, and that's how the family got ahead.

I do not celebrate that today's couples are breaking the mold, because the cause is too often the malfunction of our economic system, and the resulting household dynamics are equally untenable. Instead of a healthy middle class we have a higher upper class and a larger lower class. In wealthy homes, the spouses are more free to coordinate their gender affect—they can grunge out and tackle chores together, then get dressed up for companionable recreation. But more families are falling behind financially than stepping up to that kind of freedom. In these, everyone is grubbing for existence together, and no one ever feels fully empowered or confident that the path they are on will result in a better future. Meanwhile, old stereotypes die hard, and I think it is safe to say that when there is a man in the household, he is the one feeling the greatest burden and shame of economic failure. No, I would not want to be a guy. Especially not these days when the cards are stacked against workers.

Not succeeding as a breadwinner? How about trying out for a superhero role? Not me. Fictional portrayals of manly heroism are over the top in the levels of violence both endured and dished out. Meanwhile, real threats of natural disaster, crime, war and terrorism are hyped so vividly and insistently, one might expect and even desire our men to be fierce and ready for action, yet daily social life is ever more restricted. We see institutions clamping down on boys and young men in a determined effort to tame and meeken them—as if frustrating a young person's natural self-expression could possibly be an effective curb to bullying behavior.

Before we can make room for normal, authentic exploration of our facets of personality, including sexuality and gender identification, we will have to create a setting in which that can even occur, and we're not there yet. Boys and girls are poisoned by ages-old stereotypes and expectations that are embedded in our institutions and continually reinforced by mass media. These stereotypes have been altered and manipulated over time to present an illusion of change even while the status quo is more firmly cemented.

For example, women's liberation became the sexual revolution, with the result that instead of being objectified as fragile goddesses on a pedestal, we may now be objectified as sturdy, self-volunteered sex toys. And men can be objectified too, and subjected to the same appearance-driven grading of success. No longer may guys assume that acceptance will come with a big paycheck or big muscles—now they also get to fuss with their hair, worry about flab, and wear trendy clothes. Oh joy, what progress.

In "the battle of the sexes," women look at men and see all of the opportunities to do things that we have been denied—in education, work and general social mobility. But men look at women and see all of the opportunities *not* to do things that they have been denied—all the heavy, dirty, violent, dangerous, and soul-numbing labors of traditional protector and breadwinner. It's nutty, not just because these generalizations are grossly inaccurate, but because each side sees the other as more privileged. We won't ever get it together until we get over *that*.

Being stuck in a compartment is being stuck, deprived of room to grow. Does someone else's cell look more comfortable? They're still stuck. Let's all help each other get out of this lose-lose gender war.

I wouldn't want to be a guy because I'm not a guy, I'm me. Curious as I may be about how much of "me" is nature and how much is nurture, I don't get a do-over in which to grow up in a world where gender identity is less defined and has less impact. I just have to work with what I got. All I want for myself and for all of you is that we will be free to discover our own authentic selves, reach our full potential, and connect with each other with honesty and mutual admiration.

Oh, *Now* We're Worried About
the Fourth Amendment
June 18, 2013

"The right of the people to be secure in their persons, houses, papers, and effects, against unreasonable searches and seizures, shall not be violated, and no Warrants shall issue, but upon probable cause, supported by Oath or affirmation, and particularly describing the place to be searched, and the persons or things to be seized. " Amendment IV of the Constitution of the United States of America

I don't know whether to laugh or cry. The Defenders of the Right to Privacy have surfaced. One wonders what they do when off duty, which they frequently are. Buying guns perhaps, or browsing smutty web sites. Well, it's none of your damn business, and they're coming out of the woodwork to complain about the Feds helping themselves to repositories of phone and internet metadata "just in case" they want to search it later.

I sure would like to know where the outrage was and is, Fourth-Amendment-wise, over states passing legislation requiring transvaginal ultrasounds for women seeking to have an abortion. Talk about invading the privacy of one's person unreasonably, without probable cause, and lacking any warrant— What was everyone doing when that crap came around?

Where was the Fourth Amendment teach-in when suddenly women facing an intimate, personal and emotionally charged decision found themselves subject to invasive physical and psychological probing without cause of any sort? There has been an outcry over the procedure—unnecessary, intrusive, expensive, discriminatory, demeaning, and all of that. But we've had more debate about the *privacy* of arrestees getting their cheeks swabbed for DNA than we've had about women who seek legal medical treatment being subject to a legislated physical assault. Shall we discuss the inexcusable unconstitutional overreach of local governments as they continue to introduce laws that infringe on women's authority over their own bodies and health care?

It's the Fourth Amendment, dudes. Does it apply to women or not?

Women do not want special treatment or special protection—we have seen what that looks like. We want equality under the law and we want it in writing. It's time to ratify the Equal Rights Amendment.

(Got that, Big Brother? Go ahead, meta my day.)

Born to Worry
July 31, 2013

PBS recently re-aired their two-hour program on the life of Siddhartha Gautama, *The Buddha* by David Grubin. Somewhere around here I still have a battered copy of Herman Hesse's *Siddhartha*, which can be read in about the same amount of time. It is a novel about a man who is not Gautama Buddha, but who meets the Buddha, and whose life in some ways parallels the Buddha's. I was very inspired by it back in high school. I had become fascinated by Buddhism and Eastern philosophy in general. But, like Hesse's character, I was not altogether sold on the totality of the Buddha's enlightenment. I didn't know the term at the time, but I was already working my way toward humanism.

The revelation of the Buddha, as portrayed in the documentary, can be boiled down to four words: "Don't worry, be happy." Our worries spring from the activity of our minds; when we just let ourselves groove on the wonder of *what is*, we can be joyfully at peace.

It's a good trick if you can master it. We lay people are not expected to function exclusively in this state of bliss, but at least we might know it is available through meditation, and go there periodically to restore balance. Indeed, we wouldn't have much of a functional society were everyone to devote themselves to seeking inner peace all the time. My impression of history's most celebrated spiritual and intellectual leaders is that they were either destitute or privileged. They may have been supported by their followers or, alternatively, taken care of by people in their employ or family members whom their personal wealth could support. But you will not find a lot of working stiffs in this elite club.

And so I have always had a bone to pick with the Buddha. In order to seek enlightenment, he left his wife and newborn son, and didn't look back or have a regret on *that* score for seven years. He started out in privilege, surrendered all worldly goods, then worked his way back around from asceticism to a less severe form of piety that nonetheless denied materialism. In other words, he successfully skirted that reality zone where most of us must abide of necessity. He left the daily worries of life to others. Dropping in on the wife surely would have disturbed his equanimity:

"Oh, look who's back. Mr. Don't-Worry-Be-Happy. And meanwhile, who's raising your son?"

At the end of the Buddha's seeking, he returned to the ascetics, whose path he had traveled for a time, and gave his first teachings to them. He did create a place for women in his schools and a role for them in the practice of his philosophy, which was unusual for the time (circa 500 BCE). And, what do you know, he did go back to his hometown and extended family—just long enough to swipe the kid and take off again. Go ahead and run a search for "Buddha's son" to check out the various ways this family abandonment followed by paternal kidnapping can be spun. There are just no easy answers to balancing personal freedom with devotion to family. Even the Buddha flubbed that one.

I often wonder why the words "genius" and "guru" may be applied to characters who are singularly incapable of the routine necessities and niceties of daily living. How easy for them to think deep thoughts when someone else is making their soup and washing their socks. (True, Einstein, the Buddha and Jesus didn't wear socks; but whatever they did wear, you can be sure someone else washed it.)

"Don't worry, be happy" is not the wisdom of a Jewish mother. "Be careful, do good, have fun—in that order!" is the practical philosophy I grew up with.

I am inspired by the Buddha and other spiritual and intellectual figures, but I think they all get too much credit for their supposed philosophical or psychological paths to well-being. Copping out on romantic love and family relationships is kind of cheating one's way to bliss, if you ask me. How can these characters be proper teachers or role models for the rest of us when they simply abdicated responsibilities that we take quite seriously? An objective examination of *what is* indicates that, much as we may groove on it, "the Universe" is in no way concerned with humanity. It's up to us to take care of each other.

We who were born to worry have a healthy respect for the perils of the world. If most of the things we worry about never come to pass, all the better. No, I don't think that my worrying literally prevents bad things from happening, but it is inextricably linked to feelings of empathy, compassion, responsibility and caring. My worries are for others as well as myself. Further, my immediate worries are mainly practical in nature, and as such are motivating. I am appropriately concerned about things like health and financial security, and so am spurred to take needed actions.

I do not want to go through life with a begging bowl like the Buddha did (though I worry that trying to support oneself as an artist has become sadly akin to that). I think it's wise to plan ahead a little bit, or at least look ahead.

The Buddha never put a banana in his pocket for later. He collected one meal per day in his begging bowl as he traveled from place to place sharing his teachings. He didn't worry about tomorrow. Mystics, by definition, set aside mundane concerns and put their faith in faith. They surface in times of strife to offer liberation via separating mind or spirit from physical suffering.

It's good to be at peace in one's mind, but it would be better to actually fix the problems that cause the suffering. (Bananas all around!) That is the humanist philosophy: Peace of mind comes from working rationally, constructively and lovingly to improve conditions—not from denying the problems, or accepting them as inevitable, or expecting the solution to come magically or karmicly from some higher power.

I will grant you that all of society is a superficial construction, that our minds create our reality, that nature will persist with or without humanity, that we are but specks in the vast arc of history, that "this too shall pass," and that life is but a dream. But my existence feels pretty darn real to me, and your existence feels real to me too. And I worry about us, I really do.

On Women's Equality Day, Let's Recommit to Passing the ERA
August 26, 2013

Here is the speech I gave on "Why We Need The Equal Rights Amendment" at Albuquerque's Women's Equality Day Celebration. [Declaimed would be more like it, while wearing my hair in an old-fashioned top-knot and dressed up like a suffragette. For full effect, I invite you to stand on a soapbox and read this out loud at the top of your lungs.]

Sisters and brothers, fathers and mothers, poets and politicians, students and workers, kiddies and grannies, LGBTQIA+ cousins, humanists, humanitarians and humans,

The Equal Rights Amendment is for all of us! Our constitution is not complete without it, any more than it could be complete without the Thirteenth Amendment abolishing slavery, or the Fourteenth known as the Civil Rights Amendment, or the Fifteenth that granted the vote to all men regardless of race or color, or the Nineteenth, which we celebrate today, extending that right to vote to women.

Why did we need all those amendments? Because the constitution as written applied only to a select few. It has taken centuries to amend the constitution to guarantee the rights of all people in this country, and we are not done yet. Nor will we be done until the ERA is ratified, and the law of the land specifically forbids discrimination on the basis of sex.

Until that day, the women of this country are living in a loophole. People may suppose that the Bill of Rights applies to us, but we don't have that in writing—in fact, written guarantees have been denied us at every turn. Wouldn't it have been convenient to give the vote to women back in 1870 when the Fifteenth Amendment was passed? But women's suffrage was intentionally excluded from that amendment, which reads: "The right of citizens of the United States to vote shall not be denied or abridged . . . on account of race, color or previous condition of servitude."

How easy would it have been to add "or gender" "or sex" and get everyone onto the voting rolls in a single stroke? But no—women were denied. And let's be clear: Not including women's suffrage in the Fifteenth Amendment diluted at the outset the power and the advancement that "Black suffrage," as it was called, promised for people of color. Here we enfranchised a large new group of citizens and then immediately cut their representation in half by excluding the women! It would take another 50 years before women of any color joined their male counterparts at the voting booth.

And although we have the vote today thanks to our

determined predecessors, the Nineteenth Amendment, limited to women's voting rights, is still the only language that affirms equality of the sexes under the Constitution—a document that nowhere contains the words "her" or "she" or "woman."

Equality of other rights may be implied, but will not bear the weight of law without the ERA. And those other rights—such as the rights to privacy and religious freedom—repeatedly come under attack in piecemeal fashion from one state to the next, and from one administration to the next. As of today, the rights of 51% of the U.S. population are subject to local political whim. Is that equality?

In a world in which we did not need the ERA—we would have the ERA already! In a world in which we did not have gender discrimination and hugely lopsided majorities of men in the halls of power, someone with a sharp legal mind (say an Antonin Scalia) would assert that there is no specific protection against sex or gender discrimination in the Constitution (which he did), and there would be an immediate, unanimous movement to write, pass and ratify an amendment to fix that omission. Instead, look where we are: 90 years after the ERA was proposed, people are still fighting it.

Now, I know there are many social justice advocates here today. Please consider that whatever your cause, women are half of your effort, half of your voice, half of your authority, and half of the energy that has helped you get this far. Won't you lend your voice to the overarching, game-changing effort to enshrine women's equality under the Constitution? We cannot stop now, so close, just one amendment away, from closing the circle of civil rights guarantees that will finally ensure full equality under the law for every American. Until we have engaged and empowered everyone as equal partners in this grand experiment we call democracy, we cannot realize the greatness that our Founders, bless their patriarchal hearts, *almost* envisioned.

In closing, it would be traditional for me to point to the women who fought so valiantly for equal rights, and say: "Do it for them, we owe it to them to realize their dream and finally pass the ERA." But we know what they would say to that: "Don't do it for us—do it for yourselves! We fought the good fight for You!"

And so they did. Thank you for coming out to celebrate their legacy today, and may we all recommit to finishing the task they started. Let's do it together, let's do it for each other, let's do it without delay.

ERA, ERA, ERA...

"Pro-Life" Porn Show
Comes to Albuquerque
September 23, 2013

[When you have a sound argument, you don't need to resort to insulting the opposition, but I thought it might be instructive to turn the tables on this crowd. It was, and fun too.]

A group of Operation Rescue tourist-terrorists, most of whom are men, having money to burn and time to kill, have descended on Albuquerque to get their kicks insulting and degrading local women. They gather in public places to accost young women while brandishing crude pictures. They have no interest in, or perhaps no concept of, a woman being a person in her own right, but are exclusively and obsessively concerned with female sexuality and reproductive parts.

The word "abortion" stimulates them, evoking as it does something going on between a woman's legs; and they like imagining the deaths of babies, even where no baby actually exists. They are clearly fixated on sperm, and even imbue it with a sacred quality, fearing that sperm in general and theirs in particular might be thwarted from fulfilling its ordained reproductive duty (as if that would be such a loss).

The visiting pornographers have no compunction

about the possibility that the unwilling objects of their perverse fantasies may be victims of rape or rape-incest (likely, the very words only provide greater stimulation of their misogynist imaginations), and they specifically if subconsciously enjoy using the dangerous-feeling word "abortion" to trigger talk about "rape-and-incest," thus providing still more arousingly dangerous imagery.

Now, any man who stands in a public place and accosts strangers with dirty words or nasty photos may be accused of being a pervert or mentally unbalanced or both. If these visitors to Albuquerque were flashers in trenchcoats, the average person would either ignore them or call the cops, or both—but we wouldn't provide them a booth at the State Fair in which to waggle their junk. The Operation Rescue folks should be treated like the Peeping Toms they are. There is no reason to engage in debate with them, it only feeds their fixation on aspects of women's behavior that they think men should control or dictate or impose by force, and it sets back the conversation about women's rights many generations.

This is the twenty-first century. Women are in society. Women are intellectuals. Women are workers, athletes, politicians, artists, scientists and entrepreneurs. When we are working in the home or raising children, we are doing so by choice. Husbands and fathers and dirty old uncles may not own us or sell us or hire us out or commandeer our wombs. Unfortunately, all of the latter is still the stuff of fantasy for the sexually frustrated sickos hiding their impotence behind a facade of religious piety.

It's like a homegrown hyper-hypocritical version of sex tourism, this Operation Rescue. You've got a bunch of dirty old men busing around from town to town, picketing by day and spending their nights in strange hotel rooms getting off on fantasies about wanton women having to endure unwanted pregnancies.

This is the most disgusting side show to come to town in all the thirty years I've been here. In a rational world, we'd run Operation Rescue out of town or lock 'em up and register them as sex offenders. In the United States of Men, these bullies invade communities such as ours, get a hearty welcome from the Mayor and far too little scrutiny from the media, recruit a group of religious proselytizers to gather signatures for a ballot measure to restrict late-term abortions in the city, and require our citizens to hold a ridiculously expensive election—which if won will be followed by the inevitable expensive lawsuit—for a patently unconstitutional measure. And so we are all, women and men, abused and exploited by this pack of creepy zealots whose mission is to dominate the minds of those who are sympathetic to their anti-abortion message, and to literally impose their will over women's lives and bodies. (It's kind of like vicarious rape, isn't it—forcing a woman to hold something unwanted within her body.)

The ballot question will have to do with late-term abortions, but this is what Albuquerque citizens will really be voting on: 1) Shall the municipal government presume to dictate the health care of the women within its jurisdiction? and 2) Shall the municipal government attempt to impose a religious interpretation on a private, secular matter? I really question the judgment of City attorneys, that they would allow a blatantly unconstitutional ordinance to come to a vote, while failing to eject the Operation Rescue gang for harassment and public obscenity.

Breaking Wind
October 6, 2013

I can't help it. Every time I hear mention of the series *Breaking Bad* (which has been incessant for more than a week), all I can think of is *breaking wind*. I know I'm supposed to feel like I missed the greatest thing ever to hit TV, but the hype strikes me as so much hot air.

Without exception, everyone who became a fan of *Breaking Bad* raved about its excellent writing, acting and production values. The rest of us just didn't watch. Love it or ignore it. Locally the production was a big deal, bringing jobs and stars to Albuquerque and, I'm told, portraying our city and environs with loving attention to detail. Not to mention providing innumerable fluff pieces for the paper.

Our local rag, positively *verklempt* over the demise of the show, is getting in every banner ad and column inch they can before it goes away and we all forget about it. This has caused a curious juxtaposition of actual hot air stories that feature colorful photos from our annual hot air balloon festival with fan reactions to the *Bad* series' ending, and reactions to the reactions, and reactions to the reactions to the reactions.

Spoiler alert: The show was not real. The characters were not real. No one really died. (All that died were little pieces of our souls). The lead character's obituary is not real. The newspaper that published it (twice now) is not— *Darn!* That *is* what passes for the "paper of record" in this town. I hope someone over there is working on an obituary for Journalism.

So I missed getting to see our glowing southwestern skies used as a backdrop for drug addiction, murder and mayhem. And I missed seeing actors give superb performances as junkies, hitmen and dying nihilists. And I missed the edgy, brilliant dialogue between characters I would never want to meet about gritty, tough-guy business I hope never to encounter. Everything I heard about the series' plot was a turn-off: Dying dude needs money, makes meth, kills people—

Sorry, I'm still stuck on meth—my alliterative, pun-prone mind goes right to methane—breaking bad, breaking wind. Childish, sure, but you gotta wonder about the overgrown boys who keep dishing out this nasty, violent stuff. The reason I even bother writing about it is because I would welcome something well written, well acted, well produced, gripping, thought provoking and all that—that isn't just another violence-filled story about broken, bitter, ugly characters. I'm looking for something of high artistic quality, but all I get is greed, meth and death?

I want more beauty in my life—front and center, not

as a backdrop to crime and despair. It's pretty obvious that the media is trying to wean us off beauty—and substance, and seriousness, and sensitivity. They make bad things beautiful, I suppose because they think there's no challenge to making beautiful things beautiful. Besides, in their world, beauty is the bad thing. The pleasure beauty produces suppresses the deep fear response that leads to agitation and a need for some sort of comfort or distraction, i.e. desires that drive us to shop and consume.

Breaking Bad is just one example of how TV and movies condition us to accept violence and desperation as the norm, and to give up on culture, grace and gentleness. In the contemporary cinematic oeuvre, those "nice" things may only be used to put a frame around or add a contrasting element to the main event, which must always be something shocking, brutal, macho, and either morally ambiguous or flat out bad. Bad is not broken, it's working beautifully for the entertainment industry. And if you ask me, that stinks.

Men Also Deserve Better
July 19, 2014

Genuine compassion starts with oneself, says sociologist Kathleen Barry in her book *Unmaking War / Remaking Men* (Phoenix Rising Press, Santa Rosa, 2011). Subtitled, "How empathy can reshape our politics, our soldiers and ourselves," the book explores the indoctrination of boys and men into the gender identity that she calls *core masculinity*. This aggressive-violent expression of masculinity, Dr. Barry asserts, is no more natural than the submissive-nurturing expression of femininity with which girls are conditioned.

I have written a lot about women's historic relegation to "weaker sex" status, but this book made me think about the role imposed on men in the same scenario. How would it feel to put one's life on the line for family or nation, to be expected to do so, and to risk rejection, punishment and even death at the hands of one's own community for failure to perform, if only ritually, that role? Dr. Barry deconstructs the heroic-sounding word "protector" to reveal the terrible truth at its heart. The expectation that a man will protect others *with his life* implicitly devalues his own worth. (More troubling, young men too often give their lives not for other lives, but for treasure or ideology.) Barry explores the psychological impact of teaching young men that they are "expendable."

First, men are instilled with a sense of obligation to surrender themselves to the common good or a higher purpose. They are not to spare themselves. They must be strong, meaning they must suppress or overcome the natural emotions of crisis, like fear—and compassion. They are urged to root out inner weakness. In demanding so much of themselves, is it any surprise that our protectors will be scornful of others, including if not especially those they are supposed to protect? The weakness of others is responsible for their predicament. And in the process of becoming tough enough to personally endure punishment, angry enough to mete it out, and steely enough to do either on command, empathy becomes an impediment.

The irony here is that we do not need to be stripped of our own self-esteem to serve others. We are inclined to do so naturally, because of our ability to recognize our similarities with other humans, and to imagine how it would feel to be them or to be in their shoes. By definition, empathy leaps across bounds of tribal loyalty to encompass the entire "family of man": I know what pain is, I know what love is, I know what fear is—so I can feel for you, and it makes me want to help.

However, if I have been persuaded that my own pain doesn't matter, that everything other people *fear* is my lot to *face*, that would make it harder to value the feelings of others. At the same time, a diminished sense of self-worth leaves us more vulnerable to dictatorial, sometimes sociopathic, leaders. Barry writes:

Core masculinity contains both men's expenda-
bility and their contempt for women. It requires
women's complicity in accepting men's protection,
which justifies the aggression and violence
expected of them. It is universal not because it is
in male biology, but because states and movements
require men's lives for combat. . . . Nothing is
"natural" about this type of fighting or this type of
masculinity in any culture. . . . If the masculinity of
war were natural, male aggression would just
happen on its own. Society would not have to
mount the powerful social pressure of *core masculinity* it imposes on boys and expects of men.

Aside from the obvious disadvantages that a strictly
either-or macho-femme gender model creates for
women, such as loss of status and threat of sexual
violence, there are deeper ramifications to each of us
personally. Once we reject our own assigned gender
stereotype, we find we must reject the "opposite sex"
stereotype as well. This can leave us at a loss when it
comes to rebuilding self-image and identity. How do I
create my own authentic style, and a comfortable way of
expressing gender, sexual preference and relationship
status, on a continuum with so few stations between one
cartoonish extreme and the other? Where do I pause for
a reality check?

No wonder we are seeing a movement among young
people to reject gender (as in, circle one: M or F) in
favor of self-respect and personal preference. They get

it. The battle is not between "men" and "women" but between free people and the institutions that want to regiment us.

Every generation comes up against societal expectations to conform and perform according to the standards of the day. Throughout our lives we're told we need to "go along to get along"—we'll get more of what we want in the long run if we are willing to fall into line right now. But who is setting the standard? Who is drawing the lines?

Patriarchy does not mean that while women have been subjugated, men have gotten a pass. The term refers to a hierarchical system that vests power in males, but it by no means grants power to all men equally. Indeed, it is men themselves who have been perennially tasked with girding up the authority of their leaders, at risk of their lives and for little reward. Where has all of their self-sacrifice gotten us? Or the sacrifices of the women who waited at home, or fought beside them, or fought with them?

What the women's movement is fighting for, after all, is the right for women to speak and be heard—to be taken seriously when we say, for instance, as Dr. Barry is saying, "Enough guns, enough war, enough struggle and competition. Let's try something else."

The patriarchal system reflexively suppresses our voices because such messages undermine the elitist framework on which it is built. This is why we still see so much resistance to feminism and LGBTQ rights. Our struggle amounts to a real revolution. It is being waged not by ranks of uniformed soldiers marching in lock-step, but by a colorful amalgam of mortals making every effort to become our best, truest selves, the better to love and take care of one another and the planet.

I'm Sorry I Feel This Way: A Few Thoughts for the Days of Atonement
September 30, 2014

Some of you will remember the 1970 film *Love Story*. If you are like me, you remember it with disdain for its treacly banality, and the trite catch phrase, "Love means never having to say you're sorry." It was a pop-culture sensation. I understand the appeal of the concept—that love absolves us from remorse—but I've always thought they got it backwards. If you love someone, you should care about their physical pain or emotional hurt. One can express regret for someone's suffering with or without feeling personally at fault for the situation. I have tended to use the words "I'm sorry" as simply meaning "I wish it didn't have to be this way."

The tear-jerker *Love Story* was more about fairness than love. There was a class divide between the lovers, which disguised only a little bit that the bright and hard-working young woman's opportunities, and the world's expectations for her, were limited as much by her gender as her social status. One could not call it an updated *Romeo and Juliet* exactly, because the privileged

185

young man lost his lover (to a fatal disease) but not his own life; and presumably he moved on to inherit the success that was his due, without even having to say he was sorry (or to accept an apology from his domineering father). We all cried at the end at the injustice of it.

The 1970s were full of pop-psychology fads. In addition to not having to say we were sorry, we also got to Be Here Now, and agree that I'm Okay, You're Okay. These were meaningful messages to the generations that came up during the sickening Korean and Viet Nam Wars, through the last gasp of Jim Crow, in the radioactive glow of The Bomb. None of those things were our fault; we needed to accept our circumstances and move forward to The Age of Aquarius. We were eager to Make Love, Not War.

Our awareness-raising worked. At least among ourselves we started to level the divides of race, economic class, and gender identity. This was sincere and serious business, and it is ongoing. (Our success can be measured by the strength of the backlash against it.) More pop psychology attached itself to our movement along the way. Everyone needed to take deep breaths, listen, not be belligerent, figure out "where I'm coming from" and meet each other on the other's turf. "I hear what you're saying," and "This is what I hear you saying," became strategies for putting aside one's own egocentric perspective to really listen and seek points of connection or compromise.

Now, the natural human response to imagining oneself walking in another's shoes is going to be compassion and sometimes guilt. Has something we did or said, or failed to do or say, contributed to the hardships of another? Maybe the sources of those difficulties originated long before our time, but what are we doing to allay the problems now? When I start to understand, and care (or perhaps in caring, have made an effort to understand), I sure feel like saying "I'm sorry."

But what if I don't care and/or I don't feel responsible and/or I have no intention of doing anything or changing my thinking? For these occasions we have: "I'm sorry you feel that way." I admit I have used the phrase in the past and am likely to blurt it out in the future. There are times when I really do wish I could help, but I am at a loss—all I feel able to do is express regret and sympathy. I suppose I could simply issue comforting grunts, for all that words mean at that moment.

Still, words do have meaning, or should; and having been sensitized to the lameness of "I'm sorry you feel that way," I'm back to awareness-raising, starting with my own. What does it mean to be sorry, to have regrets, to take responsibility—whether or not one is at fault? These are the questions we ask ourselves increasingly as we mature.

If the couple in *Love Story* had grown old together, I bet they would have learned to say "I'm sorry" to each other. And our "hero"—the young man who, for all of his privilege, could not save his true love—may have come to regret blowing off his father's apology with "Love means never having to say you're sorry."

Forgiveness is also a way of expressing our love, but

one cannot accept an apology that hasn't been offered. Looking back now to the saint-like female character in *Love Story*, in the context of the escalating feminist movement of 1970, I wonder if the young woman was actually uttering something she herself would have liked to hear.

Women spend a lot of time apologizing, placating, demurring and otherwise expressing a self-identity that early in life was instilled with second-class, subservient status. Our constrictions were given the guise of "modesty," which literally means to minimize one's assets or limit one's reach. In the 1970s women were increasingly asserting themselves in private and public. As they did so, they left a string of apologies in their wake, since every accomplishment felt, on some level, like a transgression. The apologies really should have been flowing in the other direction, and we knew it in our guts. If it was too much to expect a sincere "I'm sorry" to issue out of the halls of patriarchal power any time soon, the women of 1970 might at least start with a suspension of their own excessive expressions of (undeserved) guilt.

Often, saying "I'm sorry" is an invitation for another to respond in kind. Since women have been uttering "I'm sorry" for a long time while having it said to us precious little, perhaps the dying heroine of *Love Story* figured: "Screw that—rather than wait for apologies that never come, I'll just release everyone from the expectation, including myself." What was the point of anyone saying "I'm sorry" for her fatal disease, something they had no control over at all? As a smart woman consigned to lesser status, she deserved more sincere and substantial apologies than that. They were not forthcoming then, and have not been issued since. In my opinion, anyone who loves women, or loves a woman, owes us some serious apologies, not to mention reparations, for our centuries of virtual enslavement and ongoing repression.

Hmmm, I have segued into a feminist rant. Should I be sorry?

My conclusions on the "sorry" business: I think it's okay to be sorry and to say it. It is not okay to not be sorry but say you are. An insincere or condescending apology is pretty obvious—saying nothing would be better. A rote, almost unconscious "I'm sorry" doesn't help either—find something else to fill awkward gaps in conversation. Finally, if you're saying "I'm sorry" all the time and meaning it, because you really feel responsible or guilty or just deeply bad about all manner of things, it's time to give yourself and everyone around you a break. You do not need to blame yourself, and others should not have to comfort or absolve you.

Happy 5775. Let's love each other and be good to each other, so we really don't need to say "I'm sorry."

Most Cynical Ad Campaigns of 2015
December 30, 2015

Here are my top four Most Cynical Ad Campaigns of 2015:

"Know the gaps." Rather than demonstrate what a fine product they can offer, this insurance company opts for pointing out that all the other policies are also lacking. Note that the ads never state that they can fill the gaps (any company could, for the right price), only that they will tell you what those gaps are up front. Presumably this is so that when you do file a claim, and they decline to pay, you will have already been informed of the gap. The slogan for their next campaign will probably be: "We told you so."

"What's in your wallet?" The Huns, the scammers, the identity thieves and burglars are all coming for you, according to this credit card company. In threatening tones that mimic the inflection of muggers, movie stars tell us we should be checking our wallets. What's in *my* wallet? A very tiny fraction of what's in theirs. Why would I want to entrust it to a bunch of bullies and snobs? The tone of this ad campaign clearly conveys to me that the company wants my money—all of it—in a syndicate-type operation where the "good" bad guys are going to protect me from the "bad" bad guys. Very threatening. I've been getting a snail-mail a week from this outfit. Wanna know what's in my recycle bag?

"Win the holidays." I think this one speaks for itself. Talk about a "war on Christmas"—this is a war on all that is good and sincere in everyone's winter celebration. Plus, I had to do a search to remember what or who the advertisement's for, so that is a loser of an ad blitz on all levels. But at least it's already on its way out.

"So long, Show Hole!" No kidding. I'm outta here. Any vendor of TV programming would be wise to minimize reminders that sitting in front of a screen for hours on end is indeed a dark, boring, depressing and unhealthy hole—and it doesn't matter how vast a variety of stuff you are able to flip through. I wonder if Show Hole comes to us from the same cynics who cooked up Find the Gaps.

Definition of "cynical" from *Merriam-Webster*: "a. contemptuously distrustful of human nature and motives.... b. based on or reflecting a belief that human conduct is motivated primarily by self-interest.... cynical implies having a sneering disbelief in sincerity or integrity...." In other words, cynicism makes hypocrisy seem pretty benign.

Hypocrisy is (also from *Merriam-Webster*): "the behavior of people who do things that they tell other people not to do...behavior that does not agree with what someone claims to believe or feel."

This at least implies a collective sense of rightness and a personal sense of shame in not living up to common standards of behavior. Unlike hypocrites, cynics don't care if they appear despicable, they assume the rest of us are just the same and only waiting for some impetus to indulge our natural impulses.

In the past couple of election seasons, I've longed for more exposure and discussion of the hypocrisy of certain politicians and party platforms. With the new year we will be racing full tilt toward another election, and hypocrites are no longer my biggest concern. I suspect that I was being rather naive right along, and that some of those I accused of hypocrisy are in fact cynics who never intended to walk their talk or thought it mattered to us if they did. All folks want is to get behind a winner, right? So you do what it takes to win, and those who were for you win with you, and everyone else is a loser.

Hmm, what does this sound like? Reality TV? The numbers game we play with social media? Corporate branding campaigns? And now our politics. The same advertising machine that brings us "What's in your wallet?" and "Show Hole" is no doubt eagerly prepping political ads of the same ilk. I'll be interested to see what they come up with.

I don't think people are inherently unethical, insincere, greedy or unkind. I don't think we expect or want our public officials to be that way. A whole lot of money and creative energy is going to be spent to convince us otherwise. At least the cynics are unashamed and transparent. Noticing the cynicism of commercial ad campaigns like those I have listed is a good way to brace ourselves for what's to come.

In other words: Get ready to have your humanity insulted (even more) in 2016.

If You Kill the Dog, I'm Closing the Book
March 13, 2016

The great thing about writing fiction is that we get to make it up. For me, the only point of making stuff up is to make my imaginary worlds more diverse, hopeful, meaningful and surprising than the world I live in.

Diversity: Although I move in a variety of circles, and have the world at my fingertips via mass media and the Internet, I am not out and about all that much (if I can help it). I don't encounter that many people from other places, and certainly not from other times. When I write fiction, I want to go beyond the comfort zone of describing only those people and situations I encounter in everyday activities. Research is essential, and often sends the narrative in unexpected directions. I like reading books that take me to new places and introduce me to people in unfamiliar circumstances.

Hope: I am a hopeful person, despite being quite aware—and repeatedly reminded—of the inevitability of death and, on a grander scale, of the rise and fall of human civilizations over the course of time. Hope, in fiction, is not the promise of a happy ending, but the possibility of one. Unlike the continuous flow of reality, fiction gets to go exactly as far as the author chooses to take it. If it's done well, the reader's mind will wander, or perhaps probe, beyond the ending of the story to consider what happens next. I would like to be left wanting to think about a book more, not with relief that it's over. If hope can spring eternal in our hearts, there's no need to kill it with fiction. I do not last long with stories that seem intent on plunging me into the depths of despair.

Meaning: Meaning is redeeming. I'm not opposed to dark subject matter that exposes sordid truths about our human condition, but I expect the author to make something redeeming out of it. In real life, everyone does not triumph over adversity, and everything does not happen for a reason (that is, by design of a busybody superbeing). In fiction there is a higher power (the author), and everything does happen for a reason (or should) because there is a plot (ideally) with a beginning, middle and end (we hope).

Writers often strive to create visceral, unequivocal, unforgettable vicarious experiences of immense suffering caused by human perversity or the relentless forces of nature. By bearing witness, the artist demands com-passion, if nothing else, from the all-too-comfortable reader. But for the effort to yield a work of art—a piece so compelling that the ugliness and terror of its subject are transformed into a sort of beauty—the author must remain aware of the line between journalism and fiction. The trick is to maneuver around that terrain in a way that gives shape to the desolate landscapes of human experience. Readers who follow to the pit of despair should ultimately be able to find their way back to a more removed vantage, to see with more enlightened eyes the pattern that was always there, our place in it, and why we have to care. Redemption.

Surprise: Not shock. The fact that crime, abuse, poverty and other bad stuff are, sadly, not surprising in real life, often leads writers of fiction to resort to shocking versions of same. To get our attention they give us the worst imaginable grisly murder, fascistic terror, psychological torture, apocalyptic devastation. Shocking, yes, but we've seen it all on the big screen already, in 3D no less. Shocking is not surprising. Surprising, at this point, would be anything beyond the standard racial/gender/age stereotypes and popular genre tropes. Surprising would be when the dog doesn't get killed.

Seriously, what did the dog do? Yet, for some reason, the dog has to die. Whether an accident or intentional malicious act, sudden dog death is surely one of the most tired and unwelcome of plot devices. It's so common that I feel uneasy every time a dog shows up in a novel. If the writing isn't very good, I may skim ahead to see if the dog will be killed early on; if so, I waste no more time on the book.

Even when the writing and story are good, the slaying of a dog will cause me to give up on the book or quickly skim to the end. The author has lost me. If they can kill the dog, they can do anything—how ugly will it get from here? The killing of the dog is an unimaginative and obvious tactic to ramp up emotion in the reader, while providing motivation for whichever character will now be spurred to fierce action by the affront. I expect better. The dog doesn't deserve to die, and the reader doesn't deserve to be jerked around with shocking violence that makes us want to toss the book aside, when we were hoping for something creative and surprising that would make us want to read on.

There are other shocking-not-surprising plot twists that will cause me to abandon a novel mid-stream. Kidnapping, rape and torture, especially of women, are places I do not want to go, especially in fiction and especially when occurring purely for the convenience of the plot—that is, the victims are of no more interest or concern to the author (and often less) than the unfortunate dog. The fact that these crimes happen all too often in reality is not a good reason to sensationalize them in fiction. I would argue that it's all the more reason to model alternative scenarios in our stories.

Did I mention that the great thing about writing fiction is that we get to make it up? I made up my mind a long time ago that if I was going to have a plot line about sexual assault, it would be attempted assault, and the intended victim would not only fight back, but prevail. I simply prefer to read and write fiction that is better than reality, not reality made into an even nastier fiction.

While I can't claim that there is no death or violence in my prose, I give you my word that the dog is safe.

Taking Another Look at *Daniel Deronda*
August 23, 2016

I was puttering around in the studio not so long ago, steeping myself in the far left politics of *Democracy Now* as they were rebroadcasting an interview with Edward Said (1935–2003), when an unexpected literary reference caught my ear and caused me to pay closer attention to the radio. What on earth could Edward Said, noted academic and proponent of Palestinian rights, have had against George Eliot, one of the greatest English novelists of the nineteenth century? . . . Really? He says her novel *Daniel Deronda* has contributed to the rise of Zionism, the displacement of the Palestinians, and the schism between the Western and Arab worlds?

I decided I had better take a look.

And so I finally broached this lengthy novel by the author of *Middlemarch* and *Silas Marner*, among other notable works. I loved *Middlemarch*, and I had intended to read more Eliot, but the next offering on the library shelf was daunting, and not only for its size. I was reminded of the reason for my earlier reluctance when I picked up the fat volume in the library again and, again, perused the back cover of *Daniel Deronda*. Right—the "Jewish" subplot. The book gets mixed reviews for that; and I was not eager to encounter a clunky or unsavory treatment of race that might lessen my esteem for a literary idol. But now, having heard Edward Said actually diss this book by name, I was eager to see what all the fuss was about. Surely Eliot had to have gotten something right, artistically, for critics and readers to still feel so argumentative about this work.

She did. And now I am going to argue my own point, which is that Mary Ann Adams (1819–1880), a.k.a. George Eliot, was first and foremost writing about the universal plight of women.

The intertwined culture clashes explored in *Daniel Deronda*—Christian-Jew, male-female, rich-poor—are strikingly similar to those playing out today. Eliot's "enlightened" Christian characters abhorred the Jewish custom of keeping women separate from men at temple, yet they virtually enslaved and prostituted their own women within a society that kept them destitute except by support of a male family member; contemporary Western culture censures the head-covering practice of Muslim women, but we tolerate pay inequities that keep women poor and dependent.

In a nearly exact parallel to the hypocrisy of Eliot's oh-so-righteous citizens, the Republican presidential nominee suggests that a Gold Star Mother was not permitted to speak in public because of her repressive religion, as evidenced by her head covering; at the same time, he finds no fault with sexual harassment in the workplace. He and his cronies, and the media who cover them, do not notice anything unseemly or inequitable about requiring professional women to wear skimpy cocktail dresses while their male counterparts are fully covered. A woman's gotta do what a woman's gotta do, right? And in Western society women are "free" to expose themselves and thereby "succeed." Lucky us. For all of our supposed liberation and apparent social advancement, women are still routinely the targets of demeaning objectification, rape culture and sex trafficking. Keeping us financially disadvantaged is the game plan; it has been propagated by most every culture and every religion for thousands of years. Eliot got it.

Literary analysis of *Daniel Deronda*, which was first published in 1876, makes note of Eliot's fascination with Judaism, her special interest in its long historical roots, and her friendship with Jewish scholar Immanuel Oscar Menahem Deutsch. I suppose her ardently feminist philosophy is so well evidenced by her own biography that it goes without saying, but surely that had something to do with her need to probe the far reaches of history for the source of Jewish tenacity and morality. Must all societies be organized around male dominance and female subservience? Shall our fates be forever dictated by either a divine plan or stupid luck-of-the-draw, in which there are but two possibilities: having male benefactors who are decent and generous, or who are abusive and uncaring? And in either case, it's a woman's duty to submit? Says who?

In leading up to the subject of Jewish self-determination (which is not even hinted at until two-thirds into the novel), Eliot dwells at length on the unhappy choices facing her heroine, Gwendolen, a young woman with seemingly every asset except one—an inheritance. Gwendolen harbors a disdain for men and male wooing, which we come to understand, in between-the-lines Victorian fashion, is the result of disturbing experiences with her stepfather. But what is she to do? That man is out of their lives, but their assets have gone with him. Mother and sisters are dependent on relatives; and when the uncle's investments crash, all hopes rest on a prospective husband for Gwendolen.

In the context of the full novel, we can see that Gwendolen has suddenly found herself in a similar position to the Jewish characters she will later meet—forced to suppress her higher aims in order to secure physical sustenance for herself and her family. While Gwendolen's aims may seem vague and vain against the lofty religious yearnings of Jewish (male) scholars, the latter need only lower themselves to moneylending and trade in goods, whereas Gwendolen's very person is on the line. Likewise, her counterpart in the "Jewish" subplot, Mirah, has been forced to work in the theater, where she barely escapes being hired out for sexual services.

Again, the vulgar truth is dealt with through innuendo, but Eliot spares no irony in portraying how acting and singing were mainly jobs for foreigners, since being on stage was considered too crass for English women. *Ladies*, she wants us to understand, were expected to sell themselves genteelly in private.

I suppose it's more comfortable for male academics to blame Eliot for promulgating Zionism without regard for the native inhabitants of Palestine, than to acknowledge that the real villains of this story are fathers, husbands and wealthy lechers. For all of the oafish, oblivious, conceited, domineering and downright dastardly male characters who inhabit this novel, Eliot offers a single decent, rational, modern man: Daniel Deronda. He is the star of the book because he treats women with respect. He also has some significant identity issues of his own.

Finally, four-fifths through the book, we come to the nut of Eliot's argument, and mine. I think this short excerpt speaks for itself, and I will not be giving away important plot details by quoting it here:

> "I gather that [your father] opposed your bent to be an artist. Though my own experience has been quite different, I enter into the painfulness of your struggle. I can imagine the hardship of an enforced renunciation."
>
> "No," said the Princess, shaking her head, and folding her arms with an air of decision. "You are not a woman. You may try—but you can never imagine what it is to have a man's force of genius in you, and yet to suffer the slavery of being a girl. To have a pattern cut out—'this is the Jewish woman; this is what you must be; this is what you are wanted for; a woman's heart must be of such a size and no larger, else it must be pressed small, like Chinese feet; her happiness is to be made as cakes are, by a fixed receipt.' That was what my father wanted. He wished I had been a son..."

With the reference to the binding of Chinese women's feet, Eliot tips the scales already heavy with the accumulated weight of Gwendolen's torment—we are not talking about only Jewish women here, but all women.

Had there been more women in influential literary and academic positions between 1876 and, say, *now*, the legacy of *Daniel Deronda* might have come down to us differently. I found it to be an excellent read, and memorable exactly because it takes such an unusual turn. It bursts the confines of the popular novel structure of its time. Numerous critics have had their say about *Daniel Deronda*, but they have overlooked much of its significance and relevance. Eliot's primary concern was not for a possible Jewish state in Palestine, but for the sorry lot of women everywhere.

This brings me back to the subject of our current presidential campaigns: It will come as no surprise to you that *I'm with her!* What surprises me is how the media have tried to create an equivalence between Hillary's "dislikability" rating and Donald's. Seriously? *He* is disliked because he's another in a long line of bombastic misogynists, and *she* is disliked because she has been buried under their insults.

Tellingly, Hillary's "dislikability" has also been proclaimed by the far left, where the entrenched chauvinists of academia no doubt do dislike her, but instead of acting rabid they hide their bias behind a mask of nonchalance: "We're so enlightened, we don't even *notice* that she's a woman, or that she speaks to women's hopes and ambitions, or that women see her as an important change from the status quo—to *us* she's just another insider politician—tsk tsk, yawn."

Now, of course, polls reveal that the more people actually hear from Hillary the more they like her, and the more they have to listen to Donald the *less* they like him. Maybe it's not a toss-up between unfavorables, and never was. Maybe it's not about race, religion or immigration. Sounds like plain old sexism to me, same as in 1876, same as usual. But *not* same as forever, thanks to determined women like George Eliot, Hillary Clinton and so many others, plus all of the real-life Daniel Derondas who really do respect us.

Women of America, This Is What Those Good Ol' Boys Think of Us
September 15, 2016

I'm with Hillary. I'm convinced she is a genuinely good person and an exceptionally qualified presidential candidate. The Republican Party's selection of Donald Trump as their nominee to oppose her strikes me as the ultimate insult. He's a joke, a bombast—not the least bit informed, prepared or serious—and she has to somehow "compete" with him. For what? Loudmouth? He wins. Rowdiest rallies? He wins. Nastiness? He wins. Experience? She wins. Consistency? She wins. Diversity of supporters? She wins. Oh look, they're running neck-and-neck.

I doubt it. I think the women of this country intend to be treated with a bit more respect than the Grand Ol' Party has offered. The Republicans had their choice of several misogynistic candidates, ranging from the simpering, holier-than-thou type to the blowhard, throw-your-weight-around type, who had at least served in elected public office prior to throwing their hats in the ring. A few were acknowledged to be even scarier than Trump, in the sense that they were real ideologues who really believed the weird and hurtful things they spouted. Still, it would have shown a modicum of national pride to go to an experienced public servant instead of a spoiled brat to contend for the presidency of the United States on behalf of their party. Sadly, these characters were utter cowards all, unwilling to take on Trump themselves. Was it for fear of the rich man being mean to them? Or because they had no desire to pit themselves against the likely female Democratic candidate, and especially no desire to lose to her?

One wonders who among the Republican hopefuls might have come forward to fend off a Trump nomination had some other, male, candidate been selected by the Democrats. I never once thought Bernie Sanders would get the nomination, and I don't think the Republicans did either. Their response may well have been the same to Bernie—let Trump be the one to go down to defeat—but more likely they would have smelled a chance for victory and put up a more competent opponent, with a more consistent and articulate counter-ideology.

The media plays into this, of course, and we can put a similar question to the press—on the right and the left: Would the Bernie Sanders campaign have been given the same amount of attention if he had been vying for nomination against a "Democratic establishment" male? The positioning and branding of Bernie's campaign had me scratching my head: *Who's* part of the establishment in this picture? Looks to me like Hillary is the true face of the previously unrepresented masses. But the media never latched onto that little irony. They latched onto Bernie—as to a life raft.

My last question is for those of you who know that Trump is a disaster and an insult, but just aren't sure if you can "trust" Hillary: What exactly are you afraid she's going to do, eat the apple?

Conclusion: A Philosophy for Everyone
June 2018

Hoping beyond hope that we would finally elect a woman president, I was cautiously optimistic in my final blog posts of 2016. Maybe our country as a whole would acknowledge that a full one-half of the population have had no role model, no one to represent us in our highest office, ever, since its inception. Maybe the time had come for voters to change that narrative.

Did we change anything? The election was not won by the woman candidate, yet a majority of the votes cast were cast for *her*. Meanwhile, the spectacle of the campaign, truly a mass media bonanza, has been kept alive with political controversies and investigations into the legitimacy of the process and the integrity of the new regime in Washington. Once-trusted journalistic institutions, subjected to increasing financial pressures, appear to have let us down; while the new technologies that challenged the old, and which had been perceived as bypassing those establishment gatekeepers of news, culture and information, have proven to be equally vulnerable to corruption. Welcome to Democracy. The onus is on us citizens, as it has always been, to be properly informed and routinely involved with the business of our communities and our country.

We are living in a hyper-connected world. Our desire for privacy, even our understanding of privacy, is being whittled away by mass media and advertisers who are desperate for us to "share" in order to gauge our likes and dislikes. Government agencies also want to know all about us, hopefully for legitimate administrative and security reasons, but sometimes in response to over-blown threats, or to serve the ambitions of those seeking to hold or keep elected position. On a more positive note, we have been through a liberating psychological shift with regard to privacy as well. Nonconformity and casualness rule; many social taboos have fallen. We no longer have to suppress our individuality or hide our alternative lifestyles. In this more open and easy-going environment, as much as in the buttoned-down past, we need a shared ethic by which we are able to pool our knowledge and talents, yet shield ourselves from unhelp-ful distractions and unnecessarily personal judgments.

The term that comes to mind is "professionalism." It's more than a work ethic—more like a working-together ethic. Professionalism can be applied to every aspect of life, and should be now that workplace activities can be conducted anywhere. Employment, household business and recreation frequently alternate and intermingle as we interact with many people near and far through our phones and computers. Plus, we can respond to almost any media instantaneously and publicly, and we are encouraged to do so at every turn.

We may forget that our spontaneous reactions do not dissipate as quickly as they are vented—they propagate, and then linger in the virtual world indefinitely. We would be wise to show some restraint in personal communication, just as we do in a professional setting.

Professionalism is more than dedication to the job, it has a lot to do with comportment. I like to think of it as floating lightly on the surface of social interaction, as opposed to diving into the depths of interpersonal sharing. This allows us to get things done cooperatively, without a lot of intense emotion, and without judging one another. It amounts to keeping in mind the context of one's dealings with someone else or a group, and staying focused on the objective. Professional courtesy and integrity keep important tasks rolling along, and allow us to appreciate our associates for their creativity and practical know-how. This leads to our mutually encouraging each other rather than competing and tearing each other down.

In the political arena, we can set aside ideology to evaluate candidates and their parties by their level of professionalism. Our elected officials have jobs to do, after all, paid for by our tax dollars. When we elect them, we are really hiring them; and as their bosses we should demand quality service. The political parties act as our Human Resources departments. We should expect due diligence from them. Has the candidate been fully vetted for trustworthiness? Does the candidate have relevant experience? Has the candidate demonstrated the skills required for the job? In short, is the candidate qualified? H.R. managers who repeatedly, or even once, select employees who are unqualified or unfit for the job tend not to hang on to their own.

What do we expect of new hires and re-hires? Conscientious work. Basic civility. Honesty. Integrity. Elected officials are our representatives. They represent our interests in the business of our country, and they represent us to the world. Employees who offend coworkers or clients, or who bring bad press to the firm, are usually let go.

Professionalism involves mentorship—training and nurturing those who will carry on the work after us. Both major political parties, and the alternative parties as well, have failed in this area. They are always looking for new voters—to vote for the same old politicos. And they wonder why their candidates are tarred with labels like "establishment" and "status quo."

As I watch one "old boy" after another step down or get hounded out of political office due to sexual misconduct and other bad behavior, I keep thinking: Why didn't he retire a decade or two ago? I do see how someone in a job of long standing would not willingly leave their comfort zone, but there is nothing comfortable about defending discredited practices, or in exposing a laudable public career of former times to the sharp personal scrutiny that today's mass culture demands. Our public servants would serve us better if, rather than clinging to power, they would work harder to share their expertise and empower a new generation of leaders.

Make room for younger colleagues, encourage them, instruct them, boost them. That's how a legacy is made, that's how the future is made. I call it professionalism. It amounts to respect—self-respect, respect for the task at hand whatever it is, and respect for all of the helpers, observers, and consumers who are participants in that task.

The great thing about respect is that it is not a depletable resource. More for some doesn't mean less for others. I continue to hold out hope for better times, when we will all demand, and dispense, more respect for all life on the planet.

Appendix

Universal Declaration of Human Rights

Adopted by the United Nations
December 10, 1948

Universal Declaration of Human Rights

Preamble

Whereas recognition of the inherent dignity and of the equal and inalienable rights of all members of the human family is the foundation of freedom, justice and peace in the world,

Whereas disregard and contempt for human rights have resulted in barbarous acts which have outraged the conscience of mankind, and the advent of a world in which human beings shall enjoy freedom of speech and belief and freedom from fear and want has been proclaimed as the highest aspiration of the common people,

Whereas it is essential, if man is not to be compelled to have recourse, as a last resort, to rebellion against tyranny and oppression, that human rights should be protected by the rule of law,

Whereas it is essential to promote the development of friendly relations between nations,

Whereas the peoples of the United Nations have in the Charter reaffirmed their faith in fundamental human rights, in the dignity and worth of the human person and in the equal rights of men and women and have determined to promote social progress and better standards of life in larger freedom,

Whereas Member States have pledged themselves to achieve, in co-operation with the United Nations, the promotion of universal respect for and observance of human rights and fundamental freedoms,

Whereas a common understanding of these rights and freedoms is of the greatest importance for the full realization of this pledge,

Now, Therefore THE GENERAL ASSEMBLY proclaims THIS UNIVERSAL DECLARATION OF HUMAN RIGHTS as a common standard of achievement for all peoples and all nations, to the end that every individual and every organ of society, keeping this Declaration constantly in mind, shall strive by teaching and education to promote respect for these rights and freedoms and by progressive measures, national and international, to secure their universal and effective recognition and observance, both among the peoples of Member States themselves and among the peoples of territories under their jurisdiction.

Article 1.

All human beings are born free and equal in dignity and rights. They are endowed with reason and conscience and should act towards one another in a spirit of brotherhood.

Article 2.

Everyone is entitled to all the rights and freedoms set forth in this Declaration, without distinction of any kind, such as race, colour, sex, language, religion, political or other opinion, national or social origin, property, birth or other status. Furthermore, no distinction shall be made on the basis of the political, jurisdictional or international status of the country or territory to which a person belongs, whether it be independent, trust, non-self-governing or under any other limitation of sovereignty.

Article 3.

Everyone has the right to life, liberty and security of person.

Article 4.

No one shall be held in slavery or servitude; slavery and the slave trade shall be prohibited in all their forms.

Article 5.

No one shall be subjected to torture or to cruel, inhuman or degrading treatment or punishment.

Article 6.
Everyone has the right to recognition everywhere as a person before the law.

Article 7.
All are equal before the law and are entitled without any discrimination to equal protection of the law. All are entitled to equal protection against any discrimination in violation of this Declaration and against any incitement to such discrimination.

Article 8. Everyone has the right to an effective remedy by the competent national tribunals for acts violating the fundamental rights granted him by the constitution or by law.

Article 9.
No one shall be subjected to arbitrary arrest, detention or exile.

Article 10.
Everyone is entitled in full equality to a fair and public hearing by an independent and impartial tribunal, in the determination of his rights and obligations and of any criminal charge against him.

Article 11.
(1) Everyone charged with a penal offence has the right to be presumed innocent until proved guilty according to law in a public trial at which he has had all the guarantees necessary for his defence. (2) No one shall be held guilty of any penal offence on account of any act or omission which did not constitute a penal offence, under national or international law, at the time when it was committed. Nor shall a heavier penalty be imposed than the one that was applicable at the time the penal offence was committed.

Article 12.
No one shall be subjected to arbitrary interference with his privacy, family, home or correspondence, nor to attacks upon his honour and reputation. Everyone has the right to the protection of the law against such interference or attacks.

Article 13.

(1) Everyone has the right to freedom of movement and residence within the borders of each state. (2) Everyone has the right to leave any country, including his own, and to return to his country.

Article 14.

(1) Everyone has the right to seek and to enjoy in other countries asylum from persecution. (2) This right may not be invoked in the case of prosecutions genuinely arising from non-political crimes or from acts contrary to the purposes and principles of the United Nations.

Article 15.

(1) Everyone has the right to a nationality. (2) No one shall be arbitrarily deprived of his nationality nor denied the right to change his nationality.

Article 16.

(1) Men and women of full age, without any limitation due to race, nationality or religion, have the right to marry and to found a family. They are entitled to equal rights as to marriage, during marriage and at its dissolution. (2) Marriage shall be entered into only with the free and full consent of the intending spouses. (3) The family is the natural and fundamental group unit of society and is entitled to protection by society and the State.

Article 17.

(1) Everyone has the right to own property alone as well as in association with others. (2) No one shall be arbitrarily deprived of his property.

Article 18.

Everyone has the right to freedom of thought, conscience and religion; this right includes freedom to change his religion or belief, and freedom, either alone or in community with others and in public or private, to manifest his religion or belief in teaching, practice, worship and observance.

Article 19.
Everyone has the right to freedom of opinion and expression; this right includes freedom to hold opinions without interference and to seek, receive and impart information and ideas through any media and regardless of frontiers.

Article 20.
(1) Everyone has the right to freedom of peaceful assembly and association. (2) No one may be compelled to belong to an association.

Article 21.
(1) Everyone has the right to take part in the government of his country, directly or through freely chosen representatives. (2) Everyone has the right of equal access to public service in his country. (3) The will of the people shall be the basis of the authority of government; this will shall be expressed in periodic and genuine elections which shall be by universal and equal suffrage and shall be held by secret vote or by equivalent free voting procedures.

Article 22.
Everyone, as a member of society, has the right to social security and is entitled to realization, through national effort and international co-operation and in accordance with the organization and resources of each State, of the economic, social and cultural rights indispensable for his dignity and the free development of his personality.

Article 23.
(1) Everyone has the right to work, to free choice of employment, to just and favourable conditions of work and to protection against unemployment. (2) Everyone, without any discrimination, has the right to equal pay for equal work. (3) Everyone who works has the right to just and favourable remuneration ensuring for himself and his family an existence worthy of human dignity, and supplemented, if necessary, by other means of social

protection. (4) Everyone has the right to form and to join trade unions for the protection of his interests.

Article 24.

Everyone has the right to rest and leisure, including reasonable limitation of working hours and periodic holidays with pay.

Article 25.

(1) Everyone has the right to a standard of living adequate for the health and well-being of himself and of his family, including food, clothing, housing and medical care and necessary social services, and the right to security in the event of unemployment, sickness, disability, widowhood, old age or other lack of livelihood in circumstances beyond his control. (2) Motherhood and childhood are entitled to special care and assistance. All children, whether born in or out of wedlock, shall enjoy the same social protection.

Article 26.

(1) Everyone has the right to education. Education shall be free, at least in the elementary and fundamental stages. Elementary education shall be compulsory. Technical and professional education shall be made generally available and higher education shall be equally accessible to all on the basis of merit. (2) Education shall be directed to the full development of the human personality and to the strengthening of respect for human rights and fundamental freedoms. It shall promote understanding, tolerance and friendship among all nations, racial or religious groups, and shall further the activities of the United Nations for the maintenance of peace. (3) Parents have a prior right to choose the kind of education that shall be given to their children.

Article 27.

(1) Everyone has the right freely to participate in the cultural life of the community, to enjoy the arts and to share in scientific advancement and its benefits. (2) Everyone has the right to the protection of the moral and

material interests resulting from any scientific, literary or artistic production of which he is the author.

Article 28.

Everyone is entitled to a social and international order in which the rights and freedoms set forth in this Declaration can be fully realized.

Article 29.

(1) Everyone has duties to the community in which alone the free and full development of his personality is possible. (2) In the exercise of his rights and freedoms, everyone shall be subject only to such limitations as are determined by law solely for the purpose of securing due recognition and respect for the rights and freedoms of others and of meeting the just requirements of morality, public order and the general welfare in a democratic society. (3) These rights and freedoms may in no case be exercised contrary to the purposes and principles of the United Nations.

Article 30.

Nothing in this Declaration may be interpreted as implying for any State, group or person any right to engage in any activity or to perform any act aimed at the destruction of any of the rights and freedoms set forth herein.

[ohchr.org/EN/UDHR/Pages/UDHRIndex.aspx]

Acknowledgments

My sincere thanks to Luke Moy for his invaluable assistance in preparing the "Art and Religion and Science and Reason" lecture for publication, and for his astute editorial review overall.

More Books by Zelda Leah Gatuskin

fiction
THE TIME DANCER
CASTLE LARK
WHERE THE SKY USED TO BE
DIGITAL FACE
THE TWO MAGICIANS

creative non-fiction
ANCESTRAL NOTES
TIME AND TEMPERATURE

poetry
BUT WHO'S COUNTING?

art
ZELDA'S COSMIC COLORING BOOK

as Editor
CHRISTMAS BLUES: Behind the Holiday Mask
Anthology, ed. by Gatuskin, Miller, Willson

FROM FEAR TO LOVE
My Journey Beyond Christianity by Harry Willson

FEELING THE UNTHINKABLE
Essays on Social Justice by Donald Gutierrez

THE WIND WAITS FOR ME
The Art and Poetry of Van Dorn Hooker III

www.ingramcontent.com/pod-product-compliance
Lightning Source LLC
Chambersburg PA
CBHW071149260626
47162CB00003B/975